Raves for *Advisor Selling*

"I've read hundreds of sales books and most do nothing more than regurgitate the same stale information from decades gone by. It's rare to find a well designed, organized and thoughtful book that gets to the point. Advisor Selling should be a staple for any B2B salesperson's desk."
Carter McCrary, Executive Vice President, Quarri, Quarri.com

"Advisor Selling clearly defines the roadmap to sales success and is a must-read for all B2B sales professionals. Be quick to listen, focus on the customer's requirements, deliver customized solutions, follow the negotiating checklist – this approach yields trust and results! Using the principles detailed in Advisor Selling will dramatically improve your customer relationships and sales success."
Jim Micklos, SVP, Business Development Fusion Marketing, thisisfusion.com

"The authors set out a solid sales framework and a set of best practices for meeting today's new market reality - the book is a must read for any sales person who wants to upgrade their performance profile for winning in today's highly competitive business environment."
Richard Ruff, Ph.D., Principal, Sales Momentum, salesmomentum.com

"Advisor Selling sums up the essence of what it takes to go from being a good sales person to a great sales person. Great salespeople learn how to build their skill set and match it up with wisdom on how to create value for their customers. Matthew and Mark have created a playbook to guide sales professionals through the transition from being a good to great sales professionals. I am eager to take my team through the process."
Rick Hanson, Managing Director, Performance Technologies & Industrial Chemicals, Croda

"This is a book for the professional salesperson who truly desires to become a top-tier performer. It gets to the heart of the matter re what salespeople need to know, and doesn't patronize them by spending time on what they probably (should) already know. You're going to come away with an appreciation for the term "Advisor Selling" because it's going to change your entire outlook re the selling process. As the authors say, "You will get as much out of this book as you put into it. Do not skim it. Dwell in it. Practice it. Live it." If you'll do that, you're going to win big!"
Robert Terson, author of Selling Fearlessly,
sellingfearlessly.com

"Do you want to become a trusted advisor to your customers (rather than just another "account rep")? If your answer is yes, then READ THIS BOOK! Matthew Hudson and Mark Hunter are seasoned veterans that bring a witty, accessible and practical approach to interacting with your customers. If you follow this process, I guarantee you will not only increase your sales, but you will elevate the relationship quality with your customers to a whole new level. Who doesn't want that?"
Trent Wachner, PhD Associate Professor of Marketing at
Creighton University

"Advisor Selling is the missing instruction manual to modern sales success. The era of old school sales - pitching, pushing, and peddling - are over. Mark and Matthew give you the street-smart insights you need to sell more, more often and more profitably. In today's sales landscape, you're either a trusted advisor or you're irrelevant. Don't just read this book; use it, highlight it, dog-ear the pages, and take plenty of notes. Implement these great ideas and your sales will never be the same."
David Newman, author of Do It! Marketing

"Puts Salesmanship in true perspective – it's really all about life – everyone likes help in achieving things and to help others to the same end. In essence all people are salespeople even if they don't think they are. This book really puts things in perspective. A great tool for me."
Jim Deller, Southwest Solutions Group

"A lot of people talk about becoming a Trusted Advisor, Advisor Selling, shows you how to become one. If you sell B2B, this book should be part of your next sales skills training program. It's worth the price for the 3 questions you need to ask and 8 best practices of demonstrations! This is one sales training methodology that you can implement-immediately and see the impact."
Ken Thoreson, Acumen Management Group
AcumenManagement.com

"As widely recognized sales experts, Hunter and Hudson have observed countless sales calls while consulting with companies around the globe. Those first-hand experiences form the backbone of this groundbreaking book. The result is a quick-reading study that teaches you far more than just consultative selling; it shows you how to actually embed yourself fully into each of your client accounts! This book is an indispensable resource for anyone serious about B2B sales."
Jeff Beals, author of Selling Saturdays and Self Marketing Power, JeffBeals.com

"Think you're selling solutions instead of products? More than likely you're not. Mark Hunter and Matthew Hudson's new book, Advisor Selling, lays out how to become a real advisor, selling customer focused solutions instead of products, that will differentiate you from your competition, eliminate price as the deciding factor to your customers, and create a long-term, loyal customer base."
Paul McCord, President, McCord Training and Development

"Too many reps inadvertently act like peddlers, Mark and Matthew have laid out a clear plan to becoming a partner!"
Tim Wackel, www.timwackel.com

"The principles taught in this book absolutely work. It will not only help you take your selling to the next level, but it will build such customer loyalty it will keep you there."
Jennifer Shirkani, CEO, Penumbra Group and Author of *Ego vs EQ*, penumbra.com

ADVISOR
SELLING

The Art of Becoming
a Trusted Advisor

By
Matthew Hudson
and
Mark Hunter

Request for permission should be sent to:

Specific House Publishing
268 Hamrick Drive
Kissimmee, FL 34759
800.814.7998
www.specifichouse.com

Cover design by Bo Parker, Thinq Design
Text design and layout by Julia Gignoux, Freedom Hill Design

Printed in the United States of America

ISBN 978-1-934683-88-0

Library of Congress 2014911360

ACKNOWLEDGMENTS

This book would not be possible without all of those generous people who allowed us to ride along with them on sales calls. The opportunity to examine their sales lives and listen to their Customers has been invaluable to us. While there is not enough room here to list them all, we do want to acknowledge their role in this book.

Matthew would like to thank Mark for being awesome and adding his expertise to this work (and doing it with humility and humor), Jessica Nelson and Julie Sibert for their editorial support, Bo Parker (cover) and Julia Gignoux (interior) for their design help, Jennifer Shirkani for her friendship and making most of the research for this book possible, Rick Segel for his mentorship, Mark Grace for creating some great opportunities to study and learn, and lastly Brayden and Madeline Hudson for teaching me that joy comes from God and my family and not from work or books

CONTENTS

Pre-ramble

We know what you are thinking—another book on selling. We understand. We thought the same thing when we were asked to write this. But hopefully, what you find in these pages will be refreshing.

Our intent was to create a system that was easy to follow, not overloaded with lots of technical jargon, and simple to put into practice. The concepts you are going to learn here are tried and tested. We have been on hundreds of hours of "ride along" sales calls where we were able to monitor not only the salesperson, but the Customer as well. We could see what was working and what was not. And this book is the edited version of those experiences over several years in several countries.

As you read through this book, you will find that we did not give equal "treatment" to every topic. We did not set out to write the definitive work on selling. We wrote this for the professional salesperson that wants to take his or her game to the next level. In some instances, we stay high-level on a topic; in others, we do a deep dive. This "undulation" (if you will) matches our experiences in working with sales professionals. The areas that either A, people are doing fairly well, or B, the specific approach is so different by industry we focus on core principles that transcend all industries. We did not want to try and be a one-size-fits-all book, which does no one any good.

For example, we do not spend as much time on prospecting in this book as we do questioning techniques. Prospecting is a topic that is very diverse based on your industry, whereas the questioning techniques discussed here fit all industries, markets, and cultures. So, in essence, we tried to respect your prior experience and training and not fill the pages with information that may not benefit you in your industry. It's the way we would want a book to be written if we were reading, so why not do that for you?

One note about the "voice" of the book. As you read, you may see some "I" references. There are two contributing authors to this book; sometimes the stories are Matt's, and other times they are Mark's. Since we both believe the teaching (not getting the credit) is the most important part, we elected to use the term "I" as a collective "I" instead of trying to point out each time whose story it is. We hope this makes the reading easier, more enjoyable and most importantly, we hope we never draw the attention to ourselves, but instead keep the focus on helping you improve the sales profitability of your business.

ONE

THE APPROACH

If you ask the average salesperson if their company sells "solutions," most likely you will get a "yes, of course we do." But if you ask the same salesperson what "solution" they sold the last Customer, they will quickly revert to telling you about their products. You can change the name of your company, change the copy on your marketing materials, and even run a big advertising campaign to support solutions, but until everyone in the organization truly changes their behavior to selling *solutions* versus selling products, then it is all a big waste of time, money, and effort.

Why is Advisor Selling so important? Well, it's not a fad or the latest trend. It is, however, the best system to be successful in today's business climate. Through the years, we have traveled an evolution of selling — the same evolution all of your competition has followed. First, we had a product. We sold the product the traditional route — through product selling. Product selling is when the focus of the sale is the product. You sell through logic showing how your feature set is better than the other guy's. In other words, the focus is on you (the product) and not the Customer.

Through the years, we added more and more features to our products to keep buyers interested. But eventually (as everyone is doing the same thing), your product is no longer unique.

So, we moved to selling these additional features by leveraging the relationships we had developed over time. People buy from us because they like us—they like the salesperson who is asking them to buy. This is what we call "relationship" selling. It is the process of

1

leveraging the good relationships you have developed over the years with your Customers.

During the next decade, the buzzword in business became "rightsizing." This was the process of making layoffs sound less harsh and added the practice of increasing employee responsibility and workload for those who remained. Suddenly, people did not have time for the long lunches or hang out times relationships desperately need as part of their care and feeding. Each week, people found themselves running out of week before they ran out of work.

At the same time, employee productivity became under scrutiny, so did the purchase practices for companies. Instead of bonuses for increasing sales, more and more companies give bonuses for decreasing expenses. Plus, the CFOs changed the business practice from one of "relationship and trust" in the salesperson and his or her company to one of the "lowest of three bidders."

And thus the end of the relationship-selling era arrived. Those favorite Customers, who you could always count on, now said things like "I'm sorry, but we have to go with the other company because they have a better price and my boss is making me." In other words, relationship selling is a lot like dating. In fact, if you have an account built solely on relationship and not on Solutions or other tangibles, then you might hear a conversation very similar to those you hear when you are dating. You know how it goes: "It's not you, it's me. I just think we should see other people...but I still want to be friends!"

In fact, in today's business climate, you may have more "friends" than Customers. Now, there is nothing wrong with building relationships with Customers. In fact, no sales transaction will ever fully get away from this part of the sale. The point here is that if the *only* reason someone buys from you is because of a relationship, and then one of two things is going to happen. First, they leave the company and then their replacement brings in *their* "friends" to do business with instead of you. Or, as we stated above, the pressure of cutting costs (which always supersedes a relationship) will force them to either switch to a new provider or perhaps drop you altogether.

In each one of these periods, we continued to believe we were somehow becoming more sophisticated with how we went to market. We put any number of names on the styles and typically the name included using the words *Customer, solution,* and *benefit.* There is nothing wrong with these, but when we examined them closer, they all had the same basic flow. They were still essentially trumped up variations of product selling.

The number of companies and/or salespeople that are still stuck in these "old world" styles of selling is amazing. We would think people would see the lack of results and realize they need to change something. (Mostly companies react by reducing the price—not a very stable strategy.) Maybe what we're experiencing is a large swath of the sales community thinking the reason they're not successful is because they're simply not working hard enough. Admittedly, this could be an issue, but let's put that aside and look at the real problem.

It seems as if each salesperson was told they needed to start every presentation, providing the Customer with rationale as to why the salesperson is so great and why their company is a leader in their industry. This approach is nothing more than a "capabilities presentation" or feature-driven presentation, and in today's marketplace ,it simply does not work.

The Internet has done a beautiful job of killing off the merits of the capabilities presentation. In today's information-driven world, there are zero reasons why a Customer would want to hear what you—the salesperson—and your company are capable of doing. The Customer does not want to hear all of the boring details about your company and how good you think you are. If they want this information, they can get it from the web, and chances are they already did that before you arrived for the meeting.

3

We sometimes see examples of the "capabilities presentation" when an organization, such as a bank, sponsors a large event. The bank representative will at some point address the audience and more often than not, will spend five minutes droning on about the size of the bank, its performance ratios, and other assorted garbage. The information may trip the trigger of the bank rep, but it does nothing for the audience. This is a fine example of a wasted opportunity. With an audience that likely contains small business owners, do you think any of these people care about a bank's national rankings? Not a chance! In this instance, the bank—the sponsor of the event—has zero chance of picking up new Customers.

This is just one example, but the above scenario happens in a variety of other situations as well. We must keep in mind that the Customer couldn't care less about you, and if that's the case, then you need to quit talking about you and your company.

You might say there is no way you've ever done something that stupid. Well, chances are you have. In fact, we all have at one time or another. The only difference is how we do it. We may no longer refer to it as a "capabilities presentation." However, we may end up doing it under the disguise of showing pictures of our production process or sharing Customer letters extolling our quality.

This brings us to today's Customer. What is different about the Customer of today versus the Customer 10 years ago? Well, first, they are well educated. They often know more about your product from their study than you realize. As we said, websites are a great resource for study. And, with the practice of providing white papers and vivid videos and demos of products and technologies online as self-service methods, coupled with blogging and social media, we should expect that our Customers are more educated and prepared than Customers in the past.

And the level of information available to them is certainly not limited to your own website. If someone enters your name, your company, and what you sell into a search engine, it will return a massive list of information.

During a speech to a few hundred owners and CEOs of small to medium-sized businesses, I asked people to raise their hand if they typically do a search on the Internet to find out what they can about a salesperson and their company before they meet with them. Over 95% of the people in the room raised their hand. If this were the case for small business owners, why would we expect a purchasing agent or professional buyer to not do the same?

In another event, we sampled how many people looked up the salesperson on LinkedIn before the appointment. Again, the numbers were astounding. While not everyone checked up before the first sales meeting, they all talked about checking after the meeting if they liked what they heard. Customers know about us in ways unheard of even a couple of years ago. Resources like LinkedIn can let your Customer shop you and not just your product. And this is important, since the first thing you have to sell is yourself.

Our challenge is that the Customer is doing this research without us, and they are drawing conclusions that may or may not be accurate.

Salespeople also are under tremendous pressure to deliver to the bottom line. It used to be "sales cures all ills." Not anymore. While it is actually a bad business practice, we see more and more companies trying to "cut" themselves into profitability. Of course, it never works and they end up cutting themselves so deep, that they cannot recover (see definition of bankruptcy).

Cash-flow pricing simply does not work. At best, it allows the company to kick the can down the road, but at the same time, it destroys the price-value relationship with the Customer. Let's not kid ourselves—the idea of saying we'll give a Customer a discount to get them to try us and then we'll make it back up when they reorder is a disaster. This approach may work sometimes, but in the vast majority of cases, it does nothing more than create a relationship built on a discount.

Worse than the damage done to the Customer relationship is the damage done to the sales skills of the salesperson. Once a salesperson offers a discount to one Customer, they will do it again and again and quickly find themselves unable to close any sale without a discount. The negative impact on the company is that its products are quickly being commoditized.

One of the basic rules to which any salesperson must adhere, particularly if you believe in Advisor Selling, is that price can never be the reason why a Customer buys from you.

THE PRICE IS WRONG.
The Customer who is attracted primarily based on price is going to be the one who leaves on price. If the Customer cannot understand and appreciate your value proposition, then they are not a Customer you should pursue.

So, what compels a company to keep your products and services once they start doing business with you or try you out? What will ensure that your company never comes up when your Customer is sitting around the table in their "white boarding" exercise to determine ways to save money—or at least if it does, it never makes the list of things to cut?

The answer is Advisor Selling. Advisor Selling is very similar to Solutions Selling, which got its start in the early '90s by authors like Neal Rackham, who wrote the book *Spin Selling*. [1] *Solutions Selling is the process of connecting your products and services as a Solution to a Customer's goal, problem, or need.* **Advisor Selling is when you take the Solutions Selling principles to the next level. It involves the work you do before the sale and after the sale is made to embed** *yourself fully into the account, increase your depth and breadth of solutions, and build evangelists for you and your company inside the account.*

Advisor Selling is different than product or capabilities selling in that the starting point is the Customer's issue and not your product or service. It is a consultative approach that, oddly enough, will do more to build a relationship than cocktails or donuts. Why? Because if you follow Advisor Selling completely, the end result is that you become more than an account rep from a company they do business with. You become a trusted advisor—thus the term Advisor Selling.

If you are a trusted advisor, then *quickly, frequently,* and *intensely* you come to key players' minds as a *critical resource* to help their organization achieve its short-term and long-term business goals, meet its needs, and solve its problems. You will get calls asking you to solve problems that have nothing to do with you or your company, yet have everything to do with you being a trusted advisor. And a trusted advisor is more valuable than a friend in today's business world. (This is why relationship selling is quickly dying.)

At this point, many of you reading are saying, "Well, I have done it the other way and I have made it work." And to that we say, "You probably have, but how often?"

Selling is a lot like your golf game. You play 18 holes and are all over the course. Yet, you have that one shot that gets you so excited that it brings you back the next time. You know the shot—the one that looks just like they do on TV, lands right on the green, spins back toward the pin and nestles just short of the cup. The key here is that we are talking about the "one" shot of 98 that you remember. You come back next time and try again. And this time it only takes you 96 tries to get the one shot. What kind of living could you make playing golf if you only got that one "money" shot every 90 attempts?

Why would anyone use a sales approach that works one out of 90 times?

Salespeople who do not follow a systemic approach to selling and ignore best practices from others are like the person who plays golf thinking he is just a few swings away from turning pro. (By the way, only 13% of golfers in the United States actually shoot below 100 when they play by the rules, and the stats are very similar in EMEA as well. How many people do you know who say they shoot less than 100?) [2]

Advisor Selling was developed through research of the best and brightest within the B2B world, as well as through tried and true practices from some of the best selling minds. This process was not created in a vacuum. In fact, many, many hours have been spent over the years interviewing top sales performers in multiple industries to understand their methodologies. The research included interviews with Customers as well. We always want to know what makes a Customer say yes. We have been compiling our data and research over the last decade and have found that the results of this methodology of selling have been effective no matter the industry or product.

We have been on hundreds and hundreds of sales calls and "ride alongs" with reps in multiple industries, including pharmaceutical, technology, packaged goods, professional services, hospitality, fitness, wholesale, retail, and more. The fascinating thing about our personal experiences and research from all these years is the common principles among all these diverse industries when it comes to selling.

The end result of our work over the last decade is a process of compiled techniques from the best practices discovered during the research. The best way to think of Advisor Selling is:

"A sales process written by B2B sales professionals for B2B sales professionals."

This program is not intended to "replace" your current skill set; rather, it's designed to add to it. In fact, you would not have the role you do with your company if you did not possess good selling skills.

8

For some of you, the discussions in this book will be review of some core ideals you already know. But in many of those cases, you will read a story or hear about a tool and think, "I used to do this!" And you are left wondering why you stopped. So if nothing else, this book will bring back those sales skills that served you well that got replaced from your excitement about new ideas like using social media to sell. For many others, this content will be brand new and we are excited to introduce you to ideas and skills that will dramatically change your sales life. Either way, it will be a great resource tool for you to enhance your selling skills and increase your commissions—which is why we are all here!

You will get as much out of this book as you put into it. Do not skim it. Dwell in it. Practice it. Live it. If you make the commitment now to invest in yourself as a sales professional by giving this sales process 100% of your effort, we promise that you will see results in your paychecks. (And your Customers will be happier too!) Honestly, the first few times you try some of these techniques, they may not work for you; they will feel awkward. That is common. The first few times you swung the golf club, it probably did not do much for you. In fact, you have to continue to practice that swing before it ever develops into something valuable. But if you keep at it, keep trying, the club can be a powerful tool for you. And perhaps you can earn some money on the golf course as well.

But also know, this sales process, while thorough, does not contain every answer. This process, like any good sales process, is based on the fact that you come to the table armed and equipped with good selling techniques. For now, consider this a listing of best practices for you to use in your everyday sales endeavors.

Advisor Selling is broken into eight Phases. Each Phase has a series of steps within it. We use the term Phase because, as many of you know, the selling process is not rigid and structured. (Although many authors and bosses would have you believe it is.) It is fluid and nimble. A "Phased" approach allows you to move around and through the process and navigate the course your Customer sets before you. Each Customer is unique (at least they think so), and the sales process has to be capable of adapting to the individual needs of your Customer.

"Phases" does not mean you can skip over or leave out one or more of them, or pick and choose what you like. Doing so puts your ability to create a meaningful, value-added relationship with the Customer at risk.

Salespeople are quick to look for shortcuts. I remember having to deal with a major account on a regular basis early in my own sales career. Because I knew so much about them, I thought I could gloss over things. Doing that wound up costing me a quarterly bonus because what I thought was a great key account began to feel I was not delivering as they expected. By omitting things, I allowed the door to swing open to a competitor.

One other note here about this process—it involves multiple sales meetings to make the sale. We say that up front because we want to be clear about our purpose. The purpose of this sales process is to raise you to trusted advisor status with the Customer. And you cannot do that with one phone call or one sales meeting. It just does not happen that way in today's world. So, if you are looking for a process that will show you the "short cuts" this is not it.

Frankly, Advisor Selling is not designed to close the sale in one meeting. There are two reasons for this: First, the chances of closing a deal in one sales meeting are less than 11%. [3] So this means while there is a chance you will close, it's not worth focusing your sales approach on. Focus on the larger percent or opportunity. (Remember the golf score analogy?)

Second, the ultimate goal of Advisor Selling is to become a trusted advisor. Would you place your trust in someone who thought they could meet all of your goals, challenges, and needs in one hour?

We believe the ultimate process has three sales meetings:

1. To gather the relevant data. (This happens in the PRESENT Phase)

2. To present your solution and check for alignment and understanding. (This happens in the PLAY Phase.)

3. To close the sale. (This happens in the aptly named ASK Phase.)

If you're confused about the need for multiple sales meetings to close a sale, let me give you an example from my own experience. When I first began my consulting business, I was eager to close deals and my tendency was to take the first need expressed by a client and use it to close a sale. Yes, it worked to get a sale but more times than not it labeled me as being an expert in a very narrow niche—and typically a niche I didn't want to be known for.

The approach I should have been using was to slow down, engage the Customer more, and learn the full scope of their needs. Then, I would have been able to respond with a much larger and better solution to their needs.

Yes, it would have slowed the process (though only slightly), but the trade off in time would have resulted in significantly larger deals. I will say there are some industries where this approach is not the right one, but those are a very small minority.

While the Phases in this sales process overlap with these meetings in some regards, the fact is, if you take this route, you are building the foundation for your role as a trusted advisor with this account. And that is the ultimate goal of this type of selling. Trusted advisors make more money—period!

This sales process is based on the evolved principles of solutions selling. It views the sale from the Customer's point of view. *Practice, drill* and *rehearse,* and you will see results.

THE ADVISOR SELLING APPROACH

THE PHASES

PLAN
Goals → Prospects → Prioritize

PROSPECT
Research → Sales Meeting Messages

PREPARE
Agenda → Prepare Questions → Political Map

PRESENT
Interview → Listen → Your Story → Next Meeting

PLAY
Customized Solution → Maximize Profit

ASK
Business Fit → AFTO

ANSWER
Objections → AFTO

ADVISE
Educate → Evangelize

TWO

PLAN PHASE

People who fail to plan, plan to fail. You have probably heard that before and thought, "What a nice sentiment." But can you honestly say that you have heeded that message? If you were to examine the average salesperson's time, you would find that his or her day is spent like this:

- ✯ 50% Handling Issues
- ✯ 30% Selling
- ✯ 15% Email/Communication
- ✯ 5% Planning

Study after study has proven that the people who invest in the planning of their business have the least amount of issues with their accounts and the highest rate of closing deals. The scary fact about the study above is that on average, less than one-third of a salesperson's time is spent selling. And the same study found that less than one percent of the people surveyed actually spend any time working on their skills as salespeople. (4) Now, before you start patting yourself on the back and saying how great you are for not being part of that one percent, know this: of all the books sold in the United States this year, less than 10 percent of them were non-fiction books. (5) This is the category for books like this one, designed to help you improve your professional skills.

That study on book purchases also showed that of those books purchased, less than 10 percent of the purchasers will ever read past the first chapter! (Thankfully for you, you've made it beyond the first chapter!) So, we thank you for buying the book. But we will not congratulate you for it until the last page.

If you truly want to excel in sales, you need to invest time in building your craft. Athletes spend more time in practice than they ever do in games. For a soccer or football player, the ratio is almost 25 to 1. How much time in practice (preparation) do you spend before the sales call? In this case, practice can mean studying, research, call prep, and even role-play.

Take an NFL quarterback as an example of preparation. This position is the highest paid position in professional football—as it should be, due to the level of responsibility they have in winning games. If you break down what a quarterback does and how much time he is actually involved in the game, it's not very much.

An NFL quarterback is involved in typically only about 70 plays per game, and the amount of time they have the ball each play averages about 4 seconds. This means they are technically working only 280 seconds per game. Go ahead and multiply that by 20 games and you have a total working year of about 5,600 seconds—or a little over 93 minutes. Wow, now that's a great job! Work about an hour and half each year and make millions! Who wouldn't sign up for that?

Now we all know the real work the quarterback does is in getting ready for the game. It's the countless hours and days studying film, practicing, and leading others In fact, one might say a quarterback spends 60 hours in preparation for each two minutes of playing time. When we begin to look at the preparation a quarterback goes through to get ready for their "selling time," it certainly challenges us to ask ourselves if we're spending enough time preparing for each sales call.

There are three steps in the PLAN Phase of Advisor Selling:

1. **Goals**
2. **Prospects**
3. **Prioritize**

Let's talk about each one separately. But more important than the details on these three steps is this—**your Plan must be in writing**. Plans that get written down are much more successful than the plans that are only "discussed." Within the first week after reading this book, you will have forgotten almost 50% of what you read. After 30 days, you will retain only 20%. [6] So, if you rely on your mental ability alone, you will not be powerful. It's that simple. Plus, studies are now showing that the act of writing something out allows you to recall it better than typing it on a keyboard. [7]

And for those of us addicted to the mesmerizing glow of our devices in the early morning light before we get our of bed or use our devices to put ourselves to sleep at night as the last thing we do, we have fallen into the trap of access. We think that because it is all at our fingertips, we can manage it all in our heads. Nothing could be further from the truth. You need a plan and you need it in writing. How many phone numbers can you recite from memory today versus 10 years ago? Why memorize them, they are in your device. While there may be some merit to that, try going 24 hours without your device and see how well you function as a citizen.

GOALS

It all starts here. What are your goals for the quarter? Not the goals your company gave you, but *your* goals. Often times, the terms "goal" and "quota" are used interchangeably, but they are dramatically different things. Quotas are used to measure the desired outcome for the company. Goals are used to measure the desired income for the sales professional (you). When I was leading a sales team, I always used quotas to manage individual performance. If a salesperson could not meet the quota for his or her territory, then, after much coaching and training to improve, I would replace them. After all, the quota was the amount of money I (the company) needed to yield from that territory to justify the salesperson in the first place.

Goals, on the other hand, are personal. They are about your needs, wants, and desires, not the company's. While your goals should never be less than the company quota, your goal should not *be* the company quota.

We know that some of you may be working in situations where the company quota is not viewed by these principles and we feel your pain. It is difficult to work for a company that uses quotas to beat one about the head.

MORE STUFF.

One thing we have learned through the years is that salespeople are not motivated by what they earn; they are motivated by what they buy. A paycheck is a means to an end goal, like a new car or HDTV or family vacation.

Stephen Covey said the key to success is to begin with the end in mind. [8] We certainly agree. How do you know if what you are doing today is going to make you happy? The only way you know is if you start with the end. The end result is what will make you happy, so everything you do today must be designed to move you in the direction of your end result.

★ **Start each quarter by defining your goals for the quarter.** Begin with the end in mind and work back (the end being what you want to buy or do this year).

★ **Now that you know what you want, how much money (commissions, bonuses, etc.) will it take to get there?**

★ **Okay, now, what do you have to sell to get there?** This can be number of accounts, total revenue with all accounts, etc. It will vary based on your compensation plan.

⭐ **Now, how many sales meetings do you need to complete to get those sales?** By now in your career, you should know your closing average almost precisely, as well as the average number of sales meetings you need to close a sale.

⭐ **Now, how many phone calls, cold calls, direct mail letters, etc. will you have to make/do to get that number of sales meetings?**

For each of these metrics above, you now have a goal. Goals only serve you well if there are several aligned or linked together to an end result. The number one reason salespeople fail at reaching their goals is not that the number was too high—its because they only focused on the one number—total revenue—and had no *plan* to get there.

Did that last sentence hit home? It did for me. I spent many years selling only focused on the total dollar. My theory is, it will all work out in the end if I just focus on the total revenue. Sales cure all ills, right? While there is some merit to this, the truth is: the more detailed my plan is, the more likely I am to achieve it. And the real danger of believing in the "total money theory" is that it allows you to ignore the details that get you to that total dollar goal.

PROSPECTS

We view prospects in two different ways. First, there is the traditional way—new accounts with which you are not currently doing business. Second, there is new business you can be doing with existing accounts. For most salespeople, the latter is where there is the greatest potential.

There are many volumes of books and articles on the best way to prospect for your business. And since each business is unique in the way you engage your prospects, we are going to spend time on the principles to use once the prospects have been identified. We get annoyed by the "one size fits all" sales books, just like you do, so, we will not attempt that here.

However, we do want to stress the importance of the two types of prospects. The truth is, when we say prospect, the vast majority of you immediately conjure up a vision of the cold call. The person you have never seen, never had a sales meeting with (or more likely the company you want to sell to), but have no idea who to contact inside to do so. That is a fair vision, but there is also a whole other side to the equation.

The account or company with which you are currently doing business can be a prospect as well. For example, you may have sold one of your services to a health system or financial institution, but there are several other services you offer that they are not using. In many cases, it's the same company you are selling to, but a different department with a different decision maker. (Or, it could be the same decision maker, just more of your services.)

We consider these prospects as well. In fact, when planning, we make sure we have a balance of these prospects with the traditional ones. We do this for two reasons:

1. **Because these are easier to close since there is a familiarity with your company.** Even though the new decision maker does not know you, his guard is lowered because he knows you are already doing business with his company. He considers that you have been "vetted" already and passed the test. Plus, for many companies, it is a very difficult process to set up a new vendor. This prospect knows that you are already setup in their system—sometimes they will use you just to avoid the battle of getting a new vendor set up.

2. **Sales made to these prospects tend to be more profitable.** In other words, the first sale usually has some heavy margin

discounts to get in the door. But this sale should be more margin rich. However, we are not saying you will never have to discount or use your best negotiation skills to win this business (lots more on that later in the book).

From a prospect's perspective, the lower he can get your price, the smaller the risk from his decision to use your solution. So there is pressure to get the price lowered. Compare this to working with an account that already knows you and is serving as your reference. The risk is not as great for the prospect, so the pressure for discounting is not as high.

How many prospects do you need in the pipeline? Well, that is up to your goals, isn't it?

PRIORITIZE

One of the most important elements in sales success is the ability to select the right account to focus on. To use a baseball analogy, too many salespeople fall into the trap of chasing the "home-run" deal and leave the singles, doubles, and triples for the other people. While this plan may meet with success at times, it has a less than 10% chance of succeeding. When the quarter end is closing in, it will always be the singles and doubles that make your quota. The real way to meet your quota and light up the sales chart is to plan accordingly.

Examine the accounts within your territory, their attributes, potential and viability to close. The **PLAN** Phase is the process to qualify leads, identify prospects, build your pipeline, and ultimately, close deals. You may have heard of the term "heat maps" before. We use the term prospect plan; it's the same thing. This is the process of determining which accounts on your list and in your pipeline have the highest potential to close and highest potential in revenue. This is a critical territory management tool for targeted selling.

PRIORITIZE.

Prioritize by ability to close. This is the best way to ensure you hit your goals and quota.

Set your plan on which accounts you need to target for the upcoming quarter. It also allows you to maximize your time wisely by hitting accounts by geography within your territory. On one ride along, we drove for five hours and had two sales meetings. We jokingly like to call this "windshield time." But how much money does wind-shield time pay these days?

The smart sales professional plans his calls and sales meetings in three ways:

    1. Closing Probability
    2. Vertical
    3. Geography

1. Closing Probability. As referenced above, your first priority is to work on accounts that have the highest propensity or ability to close. This does not mean these are the only ones, it simply means where you place the priority. These are the sales meetings you want to have first. If you are not able to get the meeting until four weeks from now, then it's okay to do the lower probability meetings. But you start by setting the high ones first.

2. Vertical. Each vertical you work with will have a different value proposition and different messaging. Even though your product or service is the same and used basically the same between the verti-cals, the customization to their goals, challenges or needs is impor-tant. For example, how you would connect your direct mail services to a retailer would be different than how you would connect to a manufacturer who sells to the retailer. They are both selling the same shoe along the chain, but their goals, challenges and needs are different. Even though it may be only slightly different, it can make a huge difference.

3. Geography. Remember the five-hour story from above? You know why it happened this way—because the salesperson allowed it. When they made the call, the prospect said, "how about Wednesday?" And rather than re-framing to a day that fit his plan, he said, "sure." Salespeople live with the fear of rejection and when they hear a yes they take it—no matter the consequences. "I want to make the prospect feel like I am focused on them," the salesperson says. Yeah, not buying it. You were afraid they would say no if you tried to suggest another time; that's the real truth.

As you develop your plan keep in mind not just the ability to make the initial sale but the ability to generate long-term sales. We like to say the only good sale is the one that leads to the next sale. Too many times, salespeople focus on the quick win and miss out on the far bigger opportunity. The title of this book is "Advisor Selling" for a reason—because we want you focusing on the total sales opportunity, not merely making this month's or this quarter's number.

Part of planning is efficiency. We see more and more salespeople jumping all over the place from call to call, and at the end of the day, they spent more time in the car than in front of a prospect or Customer. Sure, if you have to fly in a plane to get to your territory you have more control over this. But, the majority of us can cover our territory in a car—and some of us try to do it all in one day.

Early on in my sales career, I remember getting chewed out by my sales manager for what I thought was a very dumb reason. Years later, I still remember the meeting and I remember still being steamed about it for several more days afterwards. The reason my manager was on my case was because of a very nice order I was able to make, or at least I thought it was a nice order. To him, the order may have been nice, but he wasn't going to let me know it. The problem was how I got the order.

To get the order from the Customer I had to change my entire week's schedule to give me time to make a return trip to a Customer I had just visited earlier in the week. The problem was, it prevented me from making a number of other calls I should have been making. My boss saw the issue as one of time management, or the lack of it, when it came to prospecting. Yes I got the order, but if I had stayed on my original schedule, I would have been able to make far more calls. Plus, I would have still been able to get the order, as I was due back in that same area the following Monday.

Yes, it took me a while to understand what I was doing wrong, but once I did, I was able to be far more efficient in securing new business because I was able to stay focused on my plan.

IT'S YOUR PLAN.
If you have a goal for the amount of sales meetings you have to have in a day, then you know you cannot let the prospect plan your day—that is your job.

Your PLAN is not something that changes during the quarter. There are long lead times associated with the sales cycle and, therefore, there should not be significant changes during the quarter on your plan. However, leads always come in and the first rule of planning is to assess, "How does this new lead rank in my prospect plan?" "Will this new lead move me closer to my end result or away from it?" You may think closer because of the high revenue potential, but keep in mind, the higher the revenue, the longer the sales cycle. While this is not a rule set in stone, it is a generally accepted fact.

Be careful to take this step and not be chasing too many deals at one time. A purchase decision is not something that comes quickly for the Customer. They will need care and feeding during the decision process — especially if you are trying to become a trusted advisor.

Think of it this way—you only have so many hours in the week. Do you want to spend those hours chasing new leads or closing on existing leads?

Two years ago, we decided to examine all the research we had been gathering on top-performing salespeople. This data was from multiple companies across lots of different industries. We wanted to see what the common traits were for the top performing salespeople in an organization. Were there similarities? Were there identifiable themes? The answer was—absolutely!

We will save the "The 6 Traits of Top Performers" for another book. For now, let's discuss the number one trait. It was planning. All of the top performers "flipped' the time management we saw from the typical salesperson (remember the beginning of this chapter) and made planning a priority. They spent at least one full day a quarter locked away and working on their plan. Then they spent the first hour of every morning examining their plan and checking progress. It was this consistent behavior that yielded their top performing results.

That's right, the first thing they did with their day was to examine their plan for the day/week. The first thing the Bottom Performers did each morning? (Yes, we studied them as well.) They checked their email. Other people based on emails set the Bottom Performers' agenda for the day. This is what causes us to spend 50% or more of our time "putting out fires." It's gotten so bad in sales today, that we often hear people regale their stories of their firefighting ability as if it is a good thing.

The "making a plan" and "setting goals" is something that gets overblown because people want to make it either too complicated or too unrealistic. One of the best ways to leverage the goal setting process is to review your performance at the end of each week. Your goal is to record the successes you had, both great and small. One week you may achieve big success, and another week the highlight might be as basic as reaching a person you've been trying to get on the phone. Regardless of how big or small, record your successes and then congratulate yourself.

YOUR PLAN OR SOMEONE ELSE'S PLAN.
Start your day examining your plan and not your email or voicemail. If the world did not come to an end during the seven hours you were sleeping, it will keep spinning one more hour while you control your destiny by planning.

Congratulating yourself on whatever you accomplished is huge, because it allows you to end the week feeling good about yourself. Better yet, it allows you to shift your frame of mind as you look at what you need to do the following week.

Once you've congratulated yourself, think about what your plan should be for next week. Reviewing and setting your plan shortly after you have congratulated yourself allows you to take into consideration the opportunities you feel are present. The key, of course, is to make sure the weekly goals you set for yourself fit into the bigger goals you have.

The beauty of this approach is it builds on the current state of your sales motivation. If you're feeling down, this approach works great to help pick you back up. If your motivation is high, this approach allows you to leverage it even more and attain even more success.

If you want to be seen as a trusted advisor, then you have to live as a trusted advisor. That means setting goals to hold you accountable so you can be trusted, and setting goals to allow your performance to be measured.

THREE

PROSPECT PHASE

There is no excuse for someone to say they don't have any prospects or leads. In the same regard, there is no excuse for someone to say the prospects they have aren't any good. We're way past the point where salespeople can blame someone else. The excuse salespeople use about marketing not doing their job in developing prospects holds zero water.

Today there are numerous resources available to ensure every sales-person has the prospects they need. The only thing that is missing is having a plan and then executing it. With the right plan, any salesperson selling anything can and will have what it takes to be successful with regard to prospecting.

While the last Phase (**PLAN**) dealt with putting together your list of prospects and prioritizing them into a plan for the quarter, in this Phase, you will concentrate on those prospects you outlined in your plan. Your focus now is to spend time researching the prospect and understanding his or her situation, and then crafting messaging to get the sales meeting.

There are two parts to the PROSPECT Phase:

1. Research
2. Sales Meeting Messages

25

RESEARCH

Many salespeople think they can simply go into an account and gather all the information they need to make the sale. This is not true at all. Unfortunately, this common mistake may work once and then we think we can replicate it. Research has shown the more prep that goes into the sale on the front end, the less time it takes to close the sale on the back end. Plus, the other benefit of planning research is that it allows you to maximize your sales time on the targets with the highest potential for you to meet your quota.

HIGH POTENTIAL.
Far too many salespeople spend way too much time with prospects that have zero chance of ever becoming Customers. One of the key things research does is to help direct you toward prospects that have the potential to buy.

There are several tools designed for you to use, such as the Hoover's database. But the best tools are available to everyone. Using the Internet, you can find out a myriad of information about the company you are targeting. The company's own website is usually chocked full of great info that will serve you well on a sales call. While there is important data that may not available on their website, like the current products or services they are using, how long they've been in business, etc., other information like the company's mission statement, core values, and locations is commonly available on their site.

Surprising to many salespeople is the supposed "confidential information" about prospects that can be uncovered by doing a search using a cross-section of keywords and search techniques. For example, try searching for the company name and the prospect name in the same string. Or the company name and words like: plans, news, issues, etc. When you search the company, you will get what the company wants you to see. But if you vary it with other items in the search string, you will get what other people are saying.

As we stated earlier, relationships are not dead in selling—only "relationship selling" is dead. The best way to build a relationship is through common interests and shared values. It is no different than with the people you call your friends. They got to be close to you because they know who you are (core values), what drives you (purpose statement), what your needs are, and what you have in common.

In business, it's exactly the same. Companies want to do business with companies that have shared values, common purposes, and can help meet each other's needs. (We will talk more about this in the **ASK** Phase.) When you walk into a sales meeting armed with information about the Customer that goes beyond the simple data, your chances of closing the sale are proportionately increased.

One other important part of research is viability. As we said a few paragraphs ago, there is no reason for you to spend a ton of time trying to close a deal with a company that cannot pay. Try to validate financial ability during the research step and not wait until the **ASK** Phase to find out they love your Solution, but cannot afford it or cannot buy due to financial struggles. Our Solutions, while able to save money and free cash flow within the Customer's company, are still a cost to them on the front end.

SALES MEETING MESSAGES

Once you have determined the accounts you want to focus on for the quarter in the **PLAN** Phase, it is time to set appointments with those accounts. To do this, you need to use a skill known as Sales Meeting Messages (SMM). Typically, marketing uses the term One-Minute Message, synonymous with "elevator pitch." That message tells someone what your company does in a succinct manner. This type of message is good for getting a sales meeting. Like the One-Minute Message, the SMM tool tries to communicate succinctly and in one minute or less, but the purpose here is talk about the prospect and *her* company and not about your company.

As you have been progressing through this book, the theme of "trusted advisor" is consistently woven throughout. Each time we introduce you to a skill it is with the end goal of getting you to become a trusted advisor with the Customer. So, every part of your approach needs to plant the seeds and lay the foundation for you to achieve that status. How you go about getting the sales meeting has a huge impact on this and the SMM is the perfect tool for establishing you as unique from the competitors and a consummate professional.

A SMM can be used in a variety of ways: from introducing yourself and your company, to setting up a sales meeting, to summarizing a value proposition, big idea, or individual solution. Regardless of how you use it, there are three components of an effective SMM and you **must have** all three to be successful. This is where we see many people trip up.

First, they try and make the SMM into an OMM or a marketing message about the company. That will not work. With an OMM, you are talking about you. With an SMM you are talking about them. It is a sales message about the industry you are calling on and how it and the person you are trying to get the meeting with are impacted. So, the focus is on the Customer and not your company. This is a very hard distinction for salespeople when first using this tool.

Second, if you do not use all three parts, then you do not have a SMM. It's that simple. During workshops, we typically see someone really strong on the first part or the second part, but then go "off the rails" with the last part. They start to say things like "I want to come tell you about me and my company." A good SMM can never take that posture and work.

GET A SALES MEETING.
The goal and purpose of the Sales Meeting Message is simple — get a sales meeting. Only then can you close.

The goal of the SMM is simple — get a sales meeting. It is not about selling your products or services or even yourself. It is about getting to the table where you can sit across from them and sell. In all of our years of selling and coaching salespeople, we always hear "if I could just get a meeting with them, I know I could sell them!" Rather than argue that principle, we teach them how to get the meeting.

There are three components to a SMM. They are:

1. **Situation:** This is a statement that expresses your appreciation for their situation—this should include a statistic or a "hook" that interests them and shows your genuine empathy for their unique challenges. This statistic can come from a variety of places such as trade journals, research studies, blog posts, or newspapers. They relate what is going on today in the Customer's world.

2. **Expertise:** This is a statement to demonstrate your expertise as an "advisor." You could reference an article, website, or your own experience. The purpose of the Expertise portion of your SMM is to show the Customer that you are a source of information as a trusted advisor.

3. **Invitation:** This is your opportunity to express interest in having a dialogue with the Customer about her own experience and open the door for a sales meeting. It is the part of the SMM where you "Ask for the Meeting" (AFTM).

The Situation is the setup. It states a topic or issue the Customer is facing currently. This gets their attention because you did not start with your company, you started with his or hers. For example:

> *"I was reading the latest addition of Trade Show Monthly and there was a great article about the use of mobile devices by show attendees."*

First, notice how we did not start with anything "selling"? Like "who is in charge of trade shows for your company?" You see, that method might work because you are not speaking to the person with whom you want to meet. That is something you would say to the receptionist for example. A SMM does not have the same effect on the receptionist and it is not designed for them; it is designed for the prospect.

In this example Situation, the salesperson opened with a topic she knows the Customer has already been discussing. If they are in the industry, and the trade journal is buzzing about it, it's because the industry is buzzing about it. And if you are in the industry…

Now that you have laid the foundation with the Situation (and got them thinking), you deliver a statement about your Expertise to help resolve or deal with this Situation. For example:

> *"I have been doing a ton of research in this area and have learned a lot from our existing Customers, as well. While everyone agrees they need technology, the solutions we have installed have been very different each time."*

Here you see the salesperson establishing his credibility. He is showing that he is an expert on this topic, and he has done so without the annoying "I have helped many people in your industry with similar issues" line. Also, notice that the message still stays at a higher level. Remember, the goal of the SMM is to get the sales meeting. That's it. Do NOT pitch your product or services at this point. Even if they ask you a question, try to redirect back to your goal of getting the meeting.

Finally, you ask for the meeting. Now, be careful here to use language that gives the impression you want to hear from them and not talk at them. It is this last part that gets most salespeople. They give a great Situation and Expertise and finish by saying "I would like to come show you how our company can help you blah blah blah." And suddenly all the work you did to become a trusted advisor is gone—you just sound like any other salesman. For example:

> *"I would love to get 30 minutes of your time to hear about your strategy for engaging attendees' mobile devices at your trade show events. Would Wednesday or Thursday be best for you?"*

Here you see that we clearly established the purpose of the meeting as "hear from the Customer" and not "sell to the Customer" or talk about your products. In fact, later you will learn that in the first meeting, you give very little information about your products or services. It's about the Customer and their wants, interest, needs, concerns, and desires—not yours.

This Invitation gives a completely different impression in the mind of the Customer. Remember, they see you as a salesperson—just like all the other salespeople in their lives. We are trying to get them to see you as a trusted advisor.

Also notice that the Invitation ended with an assumptive close. Would Wednesday work for you, or is Thursday better? Are the mornings better for you or afternoons? Try to avoid lines like "what time works for you?" or "when would you like to meet?" Be more direct and more specific, giving them a choice. Otherwise, you've done all this great work and then left an easy out for the prospective Customer.

DON'T LET YOUR SALESMANSHIP SHOW.
If the Customer starts to process the date or time of the meeting, he is telling you he wants to meet. He is just trying to figure out a time. It is a trial close, is it not?

Let's say that you are a tech firm selling a SaaS solution. Here is an example of a general Sales Meeting Message:

SITUATION:

> *I can certainly appreciate the demands being placed on IT today to maintain a secure environment while balancing the desire to allow employees to bring their own devices onto the network.*

EXPERTISE:

> *I was reading an article the other day that listed the current exposure for a security data breech at $48,000 per incident, with some as high as $500,000.*

INVITATION:

> *I know this is an area of concern for you, and I was wondering if we could schedule a short visit to compare notes and talk about how you are addressing this danger. Are you open Wednesday morning?*

Let's say you are a paper shredding company trying to get a sales meeting:

SITUATION:

> *I was reading in the Post today about another fine levied on a company for secure documents being left in the trash. The company was*

not aware of a new law passed recently that prohibited these types of documents from being co-mingled with standard trash.

EXPERTISE:

I know that in the last two years, I have witnessed a dramatic increase in the amount of fines being handed out by the State for not securing private information. There have also been several new state security statues put into place recently.

INVITATION:

I am sure this is an area of concern for you as well, and I would love to meet you for a cup of coffee to discuss your strategy for keeping your company protected and in compliance with the new laws.

Here is an example of a SMM to get an appointment with a current Customer:

SITUATION:

I know how hard you have been working to keep your company's costs down. The recent reductions in budgets have caused a squeeze on your ability to provide the same level of service to employees as you have in the past.

EXPERTISE:

I have seen other companies increase their ability to manage devices significantly without a lot of extra work or hassle—or even people. We are due to have a business review. Why don't we also consider discussing the way you are managing the devices in your infrastructure?

INVITATION:

I'd love to schedule 30 minutes away from the office to talk about some of your biggest challenges. I can share some of the research I have collected to see if there are some enhancements that would make sense for your business.

OUT OF OFFICE.
Leverage the ability to have the meeting with the prospect away from their office. It's amazing how a person's perspective can change when they're not immersed in the routine of their job.

A particular Customer of mine was giving me nothing but problems. Each time I would meet with him in his office, he would get sidetracked on other issues, and I could never get him focused enough to discuss the topic of the meeting.

Trying to get him away from his desk for lunch was impossible, too, as he simply didn't feel it would be a good use of time. One time, out of frustration, I asked him if we could take a tour of his operation. My goal was to use a tour of his operation as a way for me to both learn more about his business and also hopefully get him to give me more time.

The idea worked. Upon asking, he commented that he had not seen the operations for quite some time. (This was mainly because the operations were on the other end of town, while his office was in the corporate building downtown.)

Getting him on the tour changed everything. Not only did he open up with me while visiting the operations, but also the drive to and from the location provided me with the quality, focused time I was never able to get in his office.

Never forgo the opportunity to get a meeting set up in a different location. For me, it significantly changed how I worked with my buyer and the entire company.

A good SMM is used to get the sales meeting. It all starts there. If you call a Customer and ask them if you can come sell them something, they are going to say no, right? Ah, but your reply to me is, "I don't say that when I call a Customer." Well, if you call and talk about you, your company or your product, then, honestly, you just did express that you want to sell them something.

Sales Meeting Messages are designed to get the appointment. They set you apart from others in that they position you as an expert in the industry. If your company publishes white papers or sponsors studies, then you will have tons of data for a great SMM.

Another great way to use an SMM is from the research you did earlier in this Phase. Let's say you are calling on a health system and you notice that they just got a new bond election approved for expansion on their website. Your SMM could include information regarding the bond election and the fact that the strict guidelines to monitor the "spend" of the bond are a great reason to have a strong security Solution.

If used correctly, the SMM gets you in the door and gets you the meeting to sit face-to-face with the Customer and begin the sale. SMMs work just as well with existing Customers as they do with prospects. Let's say you have a Customer with one of your solutions in place. You can use a SMM to get an appointment to discuss other solutions.

SMMs also are a great tool to use on voicemail. If we are honest, many times when you call, you get voicemail and not the actual person. If you have a solid SMM, you can leave that as your message. It works.

LISTENING

A challenge with any question is being prepared for the answer and then knowing what to do with it. One of the best examples of asking a question and not listening to the answer is a time I was working with a high-performing sales rep with a company making calls on doctors' offices. I use this example because the art of asking and listening is something that not only impacts new salespeople, but salespeople at all levels.

This particular salesperson was charged with developing new relationships with doctors. Her performance was outstanding, if you were to look at her numbers and the number of new accounts she was able to open. I was looking forward to working with this super-charged salesperson and seeing the techniques she used to open new accounts first-hand.

The day could be summed up with one call that I will never forget. The two of us entered the clinic and saw a room full of patients, as well as several nurses and techs working behind the front counter. We approached the counter and the sales representative asked to see the doctor. The question she used was, "Is Doctor _____ in today?"—nothing unusual about that question. The person behind the counter responded with "No, Dr. _____ is not here. He is in the hospital." I was immediately taken back by a single word the lady said and knew instantly it seemed out of place. She said the doctor was "in" the hospital, rather than "at" the hospital.

The top-performing salesperson I was following that day clearly didn't see anything amiss with the word "in." (She later admitted to me that she didn't even realize what was said). The sales rep quickly responded by asking, "Do you think he will be back by 2 PM today?"

At this point, I could tell by the facial expression on the person behind the counter that there was a huge problem. However, the bigger problem was that the sales rep didn't realize there was a problem. The employee responded quite softly by saying, "Dr. _____ had a stroke last night and he's not expected to make it." To say the sales rep was shocked would be putting it mildly. For a moment, I thought she was going to need to be hospitalized herself.

She was completely blindsided by the response and couldn't even begin to find the words to say. I found myself expressing sympathy on behalf of both the salesperson and myself. What surprised me most about the whole situation is how this salesperson—who was so good—did not pick up on what the employee of the clinic first told us.

The story is tragic and my heart goes out to the doctor, his family, and his employees. I wish I knew how things turned out for everyone involved (unfortunately, I don't). What I do know is the sales rep—*a veteran of the industry who thought she knew everything and could sell to anyone*—had been totally taken out of her game. A hard lesson? Yes indeed, but it demonstrates the problem we could all encounter if we are not diligent in knowing how to ask questions and, more importantly, how to listen.

If you are going to do SMMs right, you need to craft them as part of your Prospecting phase. A best practice is to spend a morning writing five SMMs for each vertical you are selling into. Remember, one SMM does NOT fit all. It needs to be tailored to the vertical and to the Customer. However, there are common themes that make the content relevant to anyone within that vertical.

CREATE SMMS BY VERTICAL.
Remember, each account is unique and each vertical is unique. Craft your SMMs to relate to the vertical's current business climate.

Over the years, we have noticed that once we have our SMMs down, we use them in lots of places. I have used them at tradeshows, networking events, over voicemail, in email, in direct marketing letters—even within my own company to get a meeting with an executive to help further my own cause.

You will find that once you have crafted several SMMs, you can use them over and over again. But be on the lookout for new material at all times. For example, try approaching your next sales training event with your company or an industry seminar as a way to find new material for your SMMs. The statistic or hook you are looking for is often discovered in these meetings.

Personally, I use a news aggregator (Pulse) every morning to search for SMM material for my business. Pulse allows me to select certain themes or topics I am interested in, and finds relevant articles or posts for me. Similar to using Google alerts (which I also use), this is combing media for conversations being held on your topic. Nothing is more powerful than when I can say to a prospect or Customer "I was reading the *Huffington Post* this morning and..."

PURCHASE PATH

Another consideration in this Phase is the way a Customer buys or receives their products and services. For example, it might not be through an outsourced provider. It might be through another channel source, such as reseller like CDW. Or, as is the case in the Federal space, they might use an expediter (reseller/integrator) to handle the sale. Whatever process the Customer follows, it is your job to align with *their* process, and not the other way around.

Too many times, we go into the sale thinking we can "change" the Customer's mind on this part of the equation. In other words, you believe you can get them to purchase it through your methods. What happens is, you spend a lot of valuable time getting them to say "yes," and then lose it all at the finish line.

One time, we had a client that wanted us to create online sales training for the retailers who sold their products. They would pay for it, and the retailers could access it for free. Sounds like a great idea, right? It was, except that all of the retailers did not allow Internet access to their employees, so there was no way to get it done. We highlighted this early and tried to get them to address the issue, but the client was determined. Anyway, you can imagine how that story ends.

TRUSTED ADVISOR.

If you want to become a trusted advisor, you will be the one "salesperson" in their lives who is easy to deal with, who accommodates their needs, and does not force them into a system or process with which they are not comfortable. Follow their path for purchase whenever possible.

Defining your approach also includes determining who needs to be in the first sales meeting you have with the Customer. Do you have a partner sales rep with you? Do you go in alone? Who from your company should be in the meeting? Who from the prospect's company? You will use all tactics. The key is to choose the best approach that has the highest propensity for success for you.

FOUR

PREPARE PHASE

Now that you have set your targets, done your research, got an appointment through your Sales Meeting Messaging (SMM), and defined your approach with this account, the next Phase is to **PREPARE** for the initial sales meeting.

Our research shows a direct correlation between the amount of time spent preparing for the sales meeting and the successful outcome of the sales meeting. [9]

There are three things you need to do in the PREPARE Phase:

1. Create an Agenda
2. Prepare Your Questions
3. Build Your Political Map

CREATE AN AGENDA

One of the biggest challenges facing a sales professional is the ability to control the meeting with the Customer. One of the key ways we maintain this control is by using an agenda for our meeting. Agendas tell the Customer that you value their time and that you are a professional "consultant" rather than a salesperson. Customers get inundated everyday by salespeople. They don't need any more salespeople. But, they could always use a trusted advisor, which is what Advisor Selling will ultimately lead you to be.

PLAN AHEAD.
Planning ahead—with an agenda—ensures that you'll be there at (and making best use of) a time that's convenient for your Customer.

It's also important to consider how your Customer prefers to communicate. Do they prefer phone or email? You can never assume. I have a Customer who prefers Twitter. If I want to talk to them, I have to send a DM on Twitter. If this is your first sales meeting, ask the Customer how they prefer to communicate.

First, create your agenda in your CRM tool (if your company is using one) when you create your calendar invite for the Customer. Sending the Customer the agenda in this professional manner will begin to position you in a different light than the other salespeople with whom they interact.

"What if they are an existing Customer?" Even better! If you recall our discussion on "relationships" in the introduction section, you will remember that if we do not constantly evolve the relationship with the Customer, then it grows stale (just like the donuts). Adding this new approach will be the fresh activity you need to help grow the relationship.

An agenda should include the following:
* ☆ Date and Time of Meeting
* ☆ Length of Meeting
* ☆ Location of Meeting
* ☆ List of Attendees (including your people, as well as the Customer's people)
* ☆ List of Topics

There is no need to detail the time for each topic on an agenda. Sales meetings are different from others in that the Customer's responses to your questions will dictate the amount of time you spend at each part.

E-mail the agenda well in advance of your meeting. This gives your Customer the opportunity to see (and get excited!) about your meeting. This also gives him the opportunity to add any additional agenda items to the meeting. If your meeting includes a demo, attach any necessary prep items that need to be completed ahead of time.

Agendas can work great with prospecting. You may have been successful with getting a meeting with a prospect for a couple of weeks out. As the date draws near, because of the travel involved, you'll want to confirm the meeting. A great way to confirm is with an agenda that highlights a couple of the key areas you'll be discussing. The agenda offers the prospect the opportunity to see that you respect their time and that you're organized. The result is fewer cancellations and better meetings.

JUST THE RIGHT AMOUNT OF INFORMATION.
When using the agenda technique for a prospecting meeting, the items you highlight should not be ones where the prospect can draw their own conclusions before the meeting.

You objective is to pique their interest even more, never give them enough to conclude that they don't need to meet with you.

If any additional people are accompanying you to the meeting (i.e. other employees from your company) attach their "bios" as well. If it is your first meeting, you might even consider attaching your photo. All this attention to detail sends a message that you value your Customer's time, and that you're providing a high ROI for their valuable time.

The true power of an agenda comes in when you are in the meeting. Too many times, a Customer can "hijack" a meeting from you and get you to "chase some rabbits" versus accomplishing your goals for the meeting.

Bring printed copies of the agenda to the meeting with you. Start the meeting by reviewing the agenda with the group. Always ask if there are any other items that need to be added to the agenda. This is especially important when you are dealing with an existing Customer. For example, if the purpose of your meeting is to gain new business, and the Customer starts asking questions about how to use products they currently buy from you, then you may spend the entire block of time discussing existing business, versus your agenda.

Remember this—the meeting will end at the determined time. This means that if you set a one-hour meeting, then it will end in one hour. Many people (Customers) schedule themselves in back-to-back meetings (the dreaded "hard stop"). This means that no matter how wonderful your meeting is going, they will leave. Even if it is just one person leaving, the attention of the rest of the group will shift. Their minds will start to wind down this meeting and begin thinking about what is next on their plates for the day. Their bodies will stay in the room, but their minds will not.

This is why it is so important to manage the time. If the Customer has an item they would like to add to the agenda, simply follow their request. Write the new item on the agenda AT THE END and say, "No problem. Let's make sure we cover the topics we originally planned for this meeting and then save time at the end to address this." This simple act will validate the Customer's request and allow them to let go of it for now and focus on the original agenda.

It's also important to note whether this new agenda item is relevant to your whole group, or just the person asking. If it is not relevant for the whole group, then consider adding it to the agenda and suggesting that you cover it with that person one-on-one after the meeting.

One other great benefit of sharing the agenda ahead of time is the audience. How many times have you been in a sales meeting, asked a question, and the prospect (Customer) said, "that's a great question! You know who you need to talk to is _____." And, of course, that person is not in the meeting. So, you have to make another trip. Plus, now the prospect has the perfect opportunity to say no—after all, there is still more information needed to make a decision.

Helpful Tips

SHARE YOUR AGENDA AHEAD.

Sharing the agenda ahead of time allows the Customer to invite others to the meeting. We have had many experiences where we arrived to the meeting and there were several people in the room—not just the person with whom we had set the sales meeting.

We even go so far as suggesting this to the Customer in our email or calendar invite, suggesting that they review the agenda and add anyone else who might need to be included.

Your time is just as valuable as the Customer's. Do not waste it or let the Customer control you due to the lack of a control tool—an agenda. Use agendas for all your meetings. It's not about how detailed the agenda is; it's the principle of professionalism that only comes from a trusted advisor.

PREPARE YOUR QUESTIONS

Preparing the questions you need to ask in advance is probably the most powerful thing you can do for your sales. While there are many great questions you could ask, you will find, when you are using a consultative sales approach like Advisor Selling, that the list of questions is much smaller.

Questions about the company's goals are just as important as ones about the department's goals. Remember, you are dealing with a director or an executive who sits in their company meetings and hears about the company goals. Imagine being able to equip them to help meet or exceed their company's goals. What power would that have for them, as an employee?

Too many times, we focus on factual or data-point questions about the account (how many employees, how often do they order, what day of the week do they like delivery) and not enough about their goals, challenges, and needs. Advisor Selling only works if you know their goals, challenges, and needs. You can know all the details about their current situation, but if you want to provide a Solution, the questions you ask need to take you there.

As you build your list of questions, keep your audience in mind. Too many salespeople fail to take this into consideration. It starts with the size of the prospect. There are two great approaches—one geared toward small companies and the other geared toward large corporations. Remember, regardless of who you're meeting with, they will have expected you to do some research about them prior to your arrival.

Naturally, it is not likely that there will be large amounts of information on the Internet about a smaller company. With these companies, you'll use what we call the "inquisitive approach" to asking questions.

Inquisitive approach is based on you asking them questions about the history of the company, how they grew, etc. Asking these questions shows interest and demonstrates to the Customer that you care about them and their business, not just as a potential Customer. The beauty of this approach is that many times, you'll be asking these questions to the owner or one of the founders of the company. Naturally, they're going to want to share their story with you. In very simple terms, you're playing to their ego. There's no better way to get a prospect talking than doing just that.

A number of times I've found myself using this approach while meeting with an owner. The next thing I know, the owner is taking me on a tour of the entire company. What makes this so valuable is while they're giving you a tour, they can't help but share great information that you'll be able to use to help serve them better. (Remember the story from earlier about getting them away from their desk?)

With the smaller company, the key is to build your questions around finding out information about them, thus the name "inquisitive approach."

A few examples of inquisitive questions include:

Tell me about how the company got started.

What were some of the issues you had to overcome to become so successful?

What's been the most satisfying part of your job so far?

What would you do differently if you started over now?

I was given a referral a couple of years ago by a friend. The company needed some help with an annual sales meeting. When I had the first sales meeting with the CEO, instead of asking details about the sales meeting, I started with the inquisitive questions, asking how he got into the business. What has been the biggest thrill so far? What has been the biggest challenge?

The conversation continued in this manner and then I asked, could you tell me about your five-year strategic plan? Where are you at on it and how is it going? (This is actually an assumptive question, which is the best approach for larger companies, but I often use them when I am dealing with the founder.)

First, I did not ask him "do you have a strategic plan?" I showed him respect by asking about his plan—meaning I gave him credit for having one. His response to my question was perfect. "We do not have one," he said. "We keep meaning to work on it, but we get sidetracked and I know that it's important." And then came the best part: "Can you guys help me with that?"

You see, by starting broad with bigger picture, inquisitive style of questioning, I can lead the conversation into areas that the typical direct or factual questions do not. You are listening for goals, challenges, and needs. In this example, rather than focusing on the specifics of the annual meeting they were planning, I took a step back and asked about bigger picture items, because I was dealing with the CEO. The same technique will work with a lower-level manager, as well. Don't forget—that person is looking to be the CEO one day, so when he is treated like the CEO, he feels respected in his position (even though he's not the big boss, yet).

For larger companies, the inquisitive approach is not the best one to use. Prior to beginning my consulting career, I worked in management for a Fortune 100 company. The last thing I would want to waste my time with was a salesperson asking me what we did. Don't waste my time! All of that could be found on the Internet, and I had far more important things to do than waste my time educating a salesperson.

When calling on a large company, you should use the "investigative approach." This means you ask questions where you show the person with whom you are speaking that you know their company and their industry. People working for large companies don't want to waste their time dealing with people from small companies. They want to deal with people like them—people who understand their business and their world.

In your research preparing for the sales meeting, you may find out a competitor of theirs just bought another competitor. A question you might ask is, "how do you intend to respond to this change?" You may have read where they just launched some new products, so you can ask them how clients are responding to the products so far. Do they like them? Are the new products working to plan, and meeting expectations?

With the large Customer, the questions you ask are built around showing them you already know something about them based on your research, thus we call it the "investigative approach."

AGENDA HELP.
Consider using your questions as topic headers on your agenda. For example, if it is a new Customer, you could use the question, "What do you see as your biggest challenges in 2015?" as the meeting subject and "Biggest Challenges in 2015" as a topic on the agenda.

Many sales processes will tell you to start with the basic questions. The Who, What, Where, and How. The problem is, these questions sound more like an interrogation than a conversation. And, a conversation is what the **PRESENT** Phase *(where you are going next)* should sound like.

So how do you get your Customer talking and telling you about themselves and their goals, challenges, and needs? The answer— stop treating this like a sales call and start treating it like a conversation (Interview).

The **PRESENT** Phase should sound like a casual conversation with friends. Prepare questions that encourage the Customer to open up and give you more than just a short answer.

Start your questions with:

Tell me about…

Give me an idea…

Why have you chosen…

Ask them to:

Paint you a picture of…

Describe for you…

Explain to you…

Walk you through…

Bring you up to speed…

Share an example with you…

Explain that again…

An easy way to look at it is: short questions will get you long answers, and long questions will get you short answers. Your objective is to get the other person talking. Don't waste this time by trying to ask complicated questions they won't understand. Keep the questions short. This allows them to more easily process the conversation and ultimately share more information with you.

Focus your questions on items you learned from your research in the **PROSPECT** Phase, and put them in writing. Nothing impresses a Customer more than to see you pull out notes and prepared questions. It's not a canned presentation or a form to fill out. You are preparing questions that will lead you to uncover their goals, challenges, and needs. You are conducting an investigation (thus the term) into the unique situation of this person and his company. Preparing the questions in advance and writing them will make a huge difference for you.

We will go into more detail on good questioning technique in the **PRESENT** Phase, but for now, focus on getting your "plan" for this first sales meeting (begin with the end in mind). The goal of any sales meeting is to gather enough information to be able to craft a solution and close the deal. Prepare all of the information you need in advance, in order to do that successfully. Never end your sales meeting (or your questions) until you have this info.

GET IT IN WRITING.

The most common thing we hear after a sales meeting is, "Oh, I forgot to ask _____." This doesn't happen when you have the questions in writing.

BUILD YOUR POLITICAL MAP

Whenever you are trying to sell into a company, the ability to know the key players and their roles is essential. While this step is in the **PREPARE** Phase, completing it actually flows through the entire sales process. Each time you have a meeting or interaction with the Customer, you will meet new people. Your job is to identify how the person you are speaking to can help you sell the account (or keep the account sold).

While there are multiple variations and categories we could place people into, we use the essential five. Each time you identify a person in the account, enter their contact information into your CRM, and as you do, check the appropriate flag to remind anyone working with this Customer who is on your side and helpful, and who is not on your side and you need to handle with care.

PLANNING TO FAIL.
Failure to build your plan will result in one of two things: No sale or a much longer road trip to get a sale.

The five roles are:

1. Decision Maker — The decision maker (DM) is the person who must sign off for the deal to go through. Be careful. Many people will call themselves the decision maker, but ultimately they really submit to someone else.

2. Influencer — This person is not the decision maker, but they have the ear of the DM and will help sell you and your solution. Also, he or she may be part of the decision-making process, but not the final authority. An example of this is a person with whom you currently work in one department who is "friends with" a person in another department that is the DM for that group. This person can make the introduction and get you in the door.

3. Coach — Not the DM, but knows the players and the corporate culture of the company. They can be used to help you decide strategy and approach to the sale. A coach is different in that they know the inner workings and politics. They are your advisors on approach and what is being said inside the company. This is different than an ally in that they are not actively selling for you. In fact, they may not be in the loop at all in this sale, but they know all the players. An ally sells for you. A Coach can sell, but more importantly, they can advise best approach with the personalities involved.

4. Antagonist — This person will work against you and your solution. He has his personal favorite (usually the competition) and wants to keep it that way. This person will work to influence the DM when you are not there. Look for ways to build bridges with this person. When in a sales meeting, see if you can get the Antagonist to publicly express something positive about your Solution.

5. Evangelist — This person is the one who becomes your evangelist inside the account. They speak highly of you, recommend you regularly, and "have your back." Hopefully, you will have DMs, Coaches, and Influencers in this category. (We will speak more about this person and their vital role in the **ADVISE** Phase.)

In the early years of my consulting business, I was eager to take on most any type of work just for the sake of keeping the business going. The problem was, in my desire to take on most anything, I never went into a sales meeting with a clear plan or objective— meaning I never had my questions in writing. I thought I was being smart by staying flexible, but in so doing I wound up never getting the Customer to focus on what they truly wanted.

The end result for me was a painful start-up, trying to land business. I would have been much better off being focused and intentional. This does not mean I wouldn't be asking the "why" types of questions, but I would have known what I was going to do with the information once I got it.

Once you have **PREPARED**, now you are ready for the sales meeting.

FIVE

PRESENT PHASE

The key to Advisor Selling is to focus on the things that interest the Customer. Every Customer listens to the same radio station: WIIFM "What's In It For Me!" But, no one cares how much you know until they know how much you care. Zig Ziglar taught us that. [10] (Or was it Teddy Roosevelt?) You must first demonstrate that you are there for them, and not just for yourself.

There are four steps in the PRESENT Phase:

1. **Interview**
2. **Listen for Goals, Challenges and Needs**
3. **Tell Your Story**
4. **Get the Next Sales Meeting**

As we have said, the key to a successful sales meeting is to start with the Customer and not with you. This is the most common trap that salespeople fall into. They lead with how great their product is and how much you need it and how it has saved others thousands of dollars (and some lives), and they forget that the Customer doesn't even care until they see how it connects to their business.

INTERVIEW

Start the meeting by having a "discovery" conversation with the Customer. We call this the Interview. This term makes sense, doesn't it? You want this to be a discussion and not an interrogation. You want the Customer to see that you (as a trusted advisor) genuinely want to know about them first.

Here are the facts: Most sales decisions are made on less than 20% of the product's feature set. [11] This means that if your Solution (and we use that word loosely here since you cannot have a Solution until you have completed the Interview) had 100 things it could do for the Customer, what makes them say yes is usually just a fraction of its capabilities (even if they like everything it does).

Think of your current Customers. When you analyze what functions they use, you will find that they probably utilize less than 20% of the capabilities. The issue is not if they use them all—what matters to them is that they like the features they do use and that it brings them real value. The Interview is where you will discover their wants, interests, needs, concerns, and desires for their department and company. It is only from listening to the Customer's answers during the Interview that we can determine which part of your product (Solution) we should discuss in the meeting. Later, when we discuss powerful demos, we will also talk about this principle— only show the features that bring value to the Customer.

The salesman will come to a sales meeting and *talk*; the trusted advisor will come to a sales meeting and *listen*. While everyone would certainly agree with that statement, lets talk about the power it gives you as a trusted advisor. First, the Customer is expecting you to come and spew features and vomit your company virtues all over their desk. They are expecting you to whip out glossy brochures or click through fancy PowerPoint or Keynote presentations. When the first think you do is Interview—i.e. ask questions and listen, you catch them off guard. They are not used to this. In fact, they find it rather refreshing. For most of the people you're going to be meeting with they spend their lives being talked to by their bosses, peers, and Customers. They rarely get the opportunity to share their opinions. So, when given the opportunity, they thrive. We all know, once you get someone talking, you get lots of great information.

Using the prepared list of questions you brought with you, begin the Interview with open-ended questions that allow the Customer the chance to share. (This should be easy since you are reading from your prepared sheet!)

BE PREPARED.
Sales Professionals who have their list of questions in writing in advance are more able to listen for goals, challenges and needs.

Earlier in the book, we talked about the problem with people still trying to deliver capabilities sales presentations. Equally as bad are presentations driven by PowerPoint, or some other form of marketing materials. A simple idea to remember is, "The best sales presentation ever made is the sales presentation never given." I first came up with that years ago, after having sat through too many stupid sales calls. Yes, I've been in sales my entire career, but along the way I've been in positions where I've had to deal with salespeople calling on me. I can't begin to tell you the number of times salespeople came to me pitching something they felt I absolutely needed, only to bore me to death.

The death becomes painful when the salesperson is doing nothing but reading the text from the presentation, or asking questions that are clearly right out of Sales 101. Whenever I found myself in these situations, I did what most Customers do—be quiet, polite, and don't say anything to hurry the person along.

One office I had was set up perfectly for me to play games with stupid salespeople. Located on the shelf directly behind where the salesperson would sit, sat a clock. I could use the clock to watch the number of minutes that would go by before the salesperson would ask me a question, or give me the opportunity to say something. The presentation should be a discussion, not a lecture!

The key is to get the Customer talking and then give them direction. You don't want a stop-start process that interrupts the flow of the conversation. Once you have them opening up to you, use questioning techniques that guide them to where you want them to go. Move them toward describing their needs, wants, desires, goals, and challenges. Remember to talk about the company goals as well as their personal or departmental goals.

Now you are ready for the Who, What, Where, How, and When questions. These questions elicit more detail and give direction to the now flowing conversation. And remember, this is a conversation, not an interrogation. These sales questions should be open-ended, and will give you information on the more general topics brought out by the opening questions. For example, "what are you looking for," "when you do that," "how important is…" These are all in response to, and focused on, the areas brought up by the Customer.

Your objective is to never allow a comment to be made by the Customer that you do not ask some form of a follow-up question about. The beauty of follow-up questions is that they allow the Customer to feel like they're in control. For you, it's beautiful because the Customer will typically share the really important information with you once they feel they are in control.

Now, you need more detail on the benefits the buyer is seeking. You want to ask open sales questions on specific subjects to start narrowing down the information. Think of the sales questioning process like a funnel. You have started with a wide-open, "conversation starting" question. Then you narrowed the possible answers slightly with the *where*, *what*, and *how* type of questions. Now you close the funnel a little more and look for more specifics. You ask questions such as, "what size," "how many," and "who else uses it."

You may have only covered one area of the needs that they gave you in response to your opening question. Think of this as one "funnel" that you have completed. If there are more needs, go back and drill down again. Do this until you have covered all of the topics related to the benefits they want that were revealed by your opening questions. After each line of questions, check your understanding of what you have heard. When you have exhausted all the benefits and needs topics, summarize and check your understanding of all the needs, wants, desires, goals, and challenges that you have discovered.

This also helps when you are ready for the **ASK** phase of the sale. You are gaining agreement on what the Customer wants, and what their goals and challenges are. If you have used solid questioning techniques, then you will set yourself up to use the most powerful phrase in selling: "Based on what you've told me."

The key to great questioning technique is not the initial questions you ask, but the follow-up or "drill down" questions. The best sales professionals know that if they can get the Customer to open up and talk, then they can find the nuggets to connect the right Solution to the Customer. It's about goals, challenges, and needs. But many times, when you ask the question, the Customer is not very forthcoming. So you need to be prepared to keep them going. Don't make the mistake of moving on to the next question just because they "answered" the first one. Many times the true answer is hidden from us until we drill down.

For example, let's say that you ask the Customer, "What are your goals for this fiscal year?" And they respond with, "Well, we really haven't set any goals. We don't work like that around here." It would be easy to think they answered that question and move on to the next one. But if you do that, you may miss the deeper issue. Instead, ask a drill-down question. "Why do you think that is?" And see where they go next. The best questioning techniques follow the Customer's responses and "direct" them to the conversation you are looking for.

THE 2 MOST POWERFUL RESPONSES.

We could list multiple questions you can use to drill down and get the Customer to open up further, but here are the two most powerful responses you must use in every sales meeting.

- ***Why?***
- ***Tell me more about that.***

I was doing some sales coaching ride alongs a couple of years ago and I had the chance to work with Madeline (not her real name, of course, although thinking back about our time together, perhaps she did not give me her real name anyway). She had been through some sales training seminars that we had conducted, and after the sessions, we spent the next couple of months riding with each salesperson to see how well they were adapting the concepts into their sales process.

We arrived at the appointment 45 minutes early. She had been following our advice. She had prepared a great agenda and sent it ahead of time, which resulted in two people being added to the meeting from the Customer. Good job. She had planned ahead and had prepared a written list of questions to ask in the sales meeting. I could tell she was nervous, so I asked her what was wrong. "The questions," she replied. "There are so many and I cut this down from what I had." I asked to see the list and sure enough, it was four pages long and we had a 30-minute sales meeting planned!

Since the list of questions was tearing her up, I decided to tear them up and that is literally what I did. (I wanted a dramatic object lesson I guess.) She went white and then red and then white again. It was a combination of terror and anger. I asked her, "Do you remember the first question?" "Yes," she replied. "Okay," I said. "Write that down on a new piece of paper. Now, I want you to write two more questions down." Can you guess what they are? "Why" and "Tell me more about that." Then I said, "You are all done. Those are all of the questions you will need."

Madeline replied, "That's crazy. The list you just tore up was much longer. What do I do with the next 25 minutes after I ask these questions? This will never work!" she exclaimed. "Why?" was my reply. And she went on to tell me why she thought this was a really bad idea. I said, "I see. Tell me more about that." And she did.

This process continued on for some time. There was a clock on the wall behind her and I was watching it to make sure we made our appointment time. But I was also timing her. When 18 minutes I passed, I stopped and said, "Okay, now do you understand?" "Understand what?" she groused. "We just had an 18-minute conversation about what you think and what's important to you and all I said was 'why' and 'tell me more about that'."

After a few moments of quiet, she looked at me and said, "You're right! That is all you said. And I told you about all kinds of stuff that had nothing to do with selling! I told you about my divorce, my kids, and my last two jobs...why did I do that?" she asked.

"I don't know," I replied. "All I said was 'why' and 'tell me more about that'. But I do know this, you kept going deeper and kept telling me more, and after awhile I think I know exactly what makes you tick."

WHY?

Next time you go into a sales meeting, write the two most powerful responses in the upper right hand corner of your pad. That way, you will always remind yourself to drill down and go deeper.

The purpose of this story is to illustrate that, while we say prepare your questions in advance, sometimes people overthink the sales meeting and over-prepare. Follow the rule of 10 questions and be sure to include the two most powerful ones.

BODY LANGUAGE

One of the ways we can leverage the power of questions is by combining them with body language. It's easy to read a book on body language, study a few pictures, and think you know everything, but we guarantee you will fail if you try that. The reason is simple: Each person, despite what we may have been led to believe, has their own personal ways they act with their body language.

As a guideline, do not take any particular body language signal to the bank until you've seen the Customer do it three times. For example, we've been led to believe that when we see a person cross their arms, it is an indication they've made up their mind, or are shutting down. The real reason a person might have their arms crossed is because they're cold. Don't rush into making fast judgments. Let the Customer guide you to what their body language signals are saying.

Before becoming a sales consultant, I held several different sales positions. In one position, I had an account that I was charged with calling on each week. From the moment I would walk into his office, the person I dealt with would have his arms crossed and would be leaning back in his chair. He maintained this position nearly 100% of the time whenever I would meet with him. Initially, I thought he was completely against me and my company, and I fought like crazy to try to get him to buy from me. My desperation reached the point that I went to my boss to ask permission to lower our prices, as I felt this was the only way I could get him to buy.

The expression on my boss' face when I asked him was priceless. He immediately chewed me out for not understanding his body language. I told him I thought I did, as I was basing my assumptions on what textbooks said. My boss then shared with me a few things about the Customer. He said because of his age, he was always cold in his office, and due to a serious injury, he had back trouble and it was difficult for him to sit up straight. Did I feel like a dummy? Yes, I did. The lesson is simple; let the Customer guide you to what their body language is saying. For this particular Customer, I learned to watch his eyes and forehead, as these were the best indicators of his level of interest or disinterest.

QUESTION LIST.
Don't get tied to the question list— focus on the Customer. Follow the Customer with your questions; do not make the Customer follow your list.

One of the most common questions I get asked when doing sales coaching is how many questions do I need for a good sales meeting? In all our years of doing this, we've never come up with the exact formula to say "if you have a one-hour meeting then you should come up with X number of questions". It's really impossible to know since it depends on the "chattiness" of your Customer. For some Customers, you are going to have to ask a lot of questions to get the information. For others, just a few.

The answer is:
However many questions it takes to get the information
you need to close the deal!

Using open-ended questions that are thought provoking and leading (investigative), like the ones you prepared in the last phase, will go a long way in getting them to open up. Plus, since the questions are broader and more opinion-based in the beginning, it's easier for the Customer to open up and talk. After all, they cannot get the answer wrong!

61

LISTEN FOR GOALS, CHALLENGES, AND NEEDS

It seems that in selling, the skills that give salespeople the most trouble are the ones that are most intuitive. For example, for us to say the second step in the **PRESENT** Phase is to listen sounds like it comes from the Harvard Business Review article on selling, entitled "Duh!" Truth be told, though, very few salespeople listen to what the Customer is saying.

It is during the Interview (when you are trying to listen) that you will be glad you prepared your questions ahead of time. The Customer will head down a side path, and then time is up. Having the questions in front of you helps serve as a gentle reminder of the data points you need to be successful.

TWO-SECOND WARNING.
One of the easiest techniques you can use to get the Customer to talk more is to wait two seconds to respond after they get done talking. It's called the "two-second pause," and it works great.

Salespeople have a huge problem with talking too much. They tend to believe the only way they're going to close a sale is by doing all of the talking. Unfortunately, according to a study by The Sales Board, 95% of Customers surveyed said salespeople talk too much. [12] The problem is, they believe salespeople really don't care what they have to say.

This is what makes the two-second pause so effective. Most Customers expect the salesperson to say something the moment they stop talking. By waiting two seconds before talking, the Customer is taken aback, and many times, will wind up talking some more. In my opinion, that's perfect because I haven't had to ask another question, yet I still got the Customer to share more information with me.

Even better, many times the best information the Customer shares with you is what they share with you *after* the pause. The reason is simple—you've allowed the Customer to feel you value what they're saying, and you have put them in charge. The outcome is, the Customer winds up sharing with you even more valuable information.

Remember, we are following a "funnel" approach with our questioning. Once you feel you have heard and/or identified a potential goal, challenge, or need, then you simply drill down from there. You will know you have heard "enough" when you can restate it back to the Customer and connect it to one of your Solutions later in the meeting.

This is your goal in listening. You are trying to find nuggets to which you can connect the Customer's words, not your words, when you talk about your company and its solutions. You are trying to get yourself in position to be able to say, "Based on what you've told me..."

TAKE NOTES.
It may seem like you are not listening when you take notes because you are breaking eye contact. But in surveys with Customers, they feel more "heard" if the person asking the questions actually cares enough to write the answers down. Don't be one of those salespeople who thinks it is impressive to keep it all in your head. It is not.

TELL THEM YOUR STORY

You will notice that this is the next to **LAST** step in this Phase. This is intentional. You never talk about your company until *after* you talk about the Customer. For most of you reading this book, this will be the part that drives you crazy. You do not present your product or services at this point.

Even if the Customer asks you a question about your products or services, resist the temptation. We have been on many a sales call when the meeting derailed because the Customer asked a question or made a statement about their needs, and the salesperson immediately "jumped all over it" and started selling. We know that's hard for you and it goes against every grain in your sales body, but its important. The minute you switch to your product, you've gone to salesman mode and away from trusted advisor status. The Customer begins to feel like everything you've done was a bait-and-switch.

So what can you talk about at this point in the sale? Tell your story. If you've been paying careful attention to what the Customer has been saying so far, you can tailor your company's story to fit what you've just heard. Your company story is not about the date your company started. Rather, it's about your company's values and how those values and beliefs align with the Customer's.

It's okay to talk about awards you have won or recognition your company has received if those awards and recognition are relevant to the current dialogue. One time, we were working with a company that had two separate divisions. On a sales call, the salesman was talking about all the awards they had won for their innovation. This might sound great, but the problem was his division—the one he was selling—did not win the awards. The Customer actually said to the salesman "why do I even care what awards you have won for what you guys do?" Granted the salesman's heart was in the right place. They believed the Customer would be impressed with his award-winning company. But since it was not relevant to the Customer's situation, it actually did more harm than good. Think of it this way: if your country wins 175 gold medals in the winter Olympics, that fact would be out of place if you were talking to somebody about the Summer Olympics.

NO.
The Customer is looking for a reason to say "no." If you stack up the features and variations of features on a Customer while Telling Them Your Story, then you are helping them in their cause to say "no."

Focus on the Customer's requirements. Your meetings should always be about your Customer's needs, rather than about what you're selling. The most important meeting you'll ever have with the Customer is the one where you gather their requirements. It's critical to get a precise and documented reading of Customer requirements. Even if you walk out of the meeting with total clarity, you will still need to send a follow up e-mail, or other written communication, to the Customer for validation. When, and only when, you receive the validation, can you then move to demonstrating how your Solution specifically meets the Customer's requirements.

If you want, you can let the Customer know that you will be taking notes, and that you will send him a copy of the notes for his review. This will ensure agreement of discussions that took place at the sales meeting. Be sure, of course, to send the neatly transcribed meeting minutes to your Customer on a timely basis! Maintain a history in CRM of all meeting minutes. They can provide the "history" you need at a future date.

It's perfectly acceptable not to have the answer for every single question you are asked. Just be sure to prepare an action list noting who will be responsible for the answer, and the date that the person will provide the information. Note, in writing, any dates and actions that are relevant to the Customer. Schedule your next Customer meeting (which should be a demo) before you leave the office.

The beauty of this entire process is that you're letting the Customer guide it. Yes, it can seem counterintuitive to what we've been taught to do in business—to lead—but it works. Let the Customer guide you. The best insights you're going to get will come from the follow-up questions you ask. It's amazing—when the Customer feels comfortable and confident with you, the salesperson, they will open up. The challenge is, many times it's not the first or even second piece of information they share with you that is so valuable. Many times, it's the third or fourth piece of information. This is why asking a follow-up question to get the Customer to build on something they shared with you can be so critical to understanding their needs.

At one point in my sales career, I had a boss that was a master at this. On occasions, he would join me on a sales call. Without fail, he would seem to magically uncover a major insight that would allow us to close the deal. One time, I asked him how he did it and his response was simple. He said his role is to merely listen and wait for the Customer to appear to be done sharing everything they intended, and then he would ask one more follow-up question regarding a specific item. Bingo! The answer to that question would suddenly unlock the vault to huge opportunities. The key is to never think you're out of questions. There is always one more follow-up question you can ask.

BE QUICK TO LISTEN.
You can't talk people into buying, but you can listen them into it. Questions are your greatest selling tool. The better you become at asking questions, the easier it will become for you to sell.

Your goal in the **PRESENT** Phase is plain and simple. Before you leave this meeting, make sure you can answer the following questions:

☆ Do I know who the Decision Makers are and will they be in the next meeting?

☆ Do I have enough factual data to complete a demo? (If applicable)

☆ Do I have specific information from the Customer that will allow me to connect my Solution to their goals, challenges, or needs?

☆ Do I know at least two critical needs they have and/or some proprietary information they have shared with me?

If the answer to the above is yes, then schedule the demo (if applicable) and move on to the last step of the **PRESENT** Phase—getting the next sales meeting.

GETTING THE NEXT SALES MEETING

Remember, Advisor Selling is not designed to close the sale in one meeting. There are two reasons for this. First, the chances of closing a deal in one sales meeting are less than 11% (and we are focused on the larger % where the money is). Second, the ultimate goal of Advisor Selling is to become a trusted advisor. Would you place your trust in someone who thought they could solve all your goals, challenges, and needs in one hour?

The fact is, if you take this route, you are building the foundation for your role as a trusted advisor with this account. And, as we said earlier, that is the ultimate goal of this type of selling.

So the next sales meeting might be the closing appointment where you share your customized Solution for the Customer or maybe it's a demo of your Solution's benefits.

Either way,
NEVER LEAVE THE FIRST MEETING WITHOUT
A DATE AND TIME FOR THE NEXT ONE.

It really is a trial close on your Solution. While they have not heard any specifics on your Solution yet, they have noticed how well you listened and took notes. And they have heard from you about your company and how it aligns with their goals, challenges, and needs.

NEXT STEPS.
Make sure your Customer is clear on next steps from this sales meeting, including any follow up that needs to happen. Leave this sales meeting with a plan for the next one—a plan towards closing the sale.

The Teaser Demo. One question we often get on sales coaching ride alongs is, "is it okay to show any part of the Solution in the first meeting?" While we have drawn a pretty hard line on listening and not selling during the first appointment, there are times (specifically in technology sales) where giving a little "teaser" of your product is beneficial to getting the next sales meeting.

However, we still shy away from this practice since it is such a slippery slope. Once you start showing any part of your product, it ceases to be a Solution and quickly turns into a capabilities presentation—which, as we have shared, is a disaster area. It is very hard to turn back once you have started down this road. As a salesperson, you interpret the Customers questions as buying signals. You get excited and show them more and more.

The problem is, at this point, it is still your product and not their Solution. The way you make it their Solution is by connecting each feature of your product to a specific goal, challenge, or need you heard from the Customer in the initial sales meeting. At this point in the process, you have not reviewed your notes or thought through a customized approach for the account, and you could risk trusted advisor status with this behavior.

So, we are not against the "teaser" demo idea, but as you can tell, we tend to avoid it to protect the power of the Advisor Selling process. If you take one thing from this book, then it would be this thought—you cannot be half anything. You are either committed and all in or not. So, if you want to use these principles, heed warnings like this one. Develop a full skill set of the sales process first, and then later—much later, perhaps, you can introduce the teaser demo. As you do, connect it to the conversation you just had.

SIX

PLAY PHASE

As it sounds, this Phase is when you determine the proper and best "play" to run with this Customer. Using your information gathered from your research and the Interview with the Customer, you make the decision on what play will have the highest success rate.

In this instance, we are defining success as the ultimate crossover point between meeting the Customer's needs, exceeding Customer expectations, and probability to Close. In this Phase, we are also using data gathered from our conversations in the **PRESENT** Phase. For example, what was the goal, challenge, or need you learned from the Customer that you can use when explaining your Solution? Or perhaps, while doing an evaluation of your product, the Customer might have commented, "I would feel more comfortable with this solution if it were _____." In this instance, the Customer is signaling that they are interested, if your Solution could do _____.

Think of the **PLAY** phase in two parts. The first part is your preparation of the ultimate solution for the Customer, based on all of the information you have gathered so far. The second part is making sure the deal you put together for this solution is good for your company, as well. A good deal for the Customer must be a good deal for your company.

There are two parts you need to address in the PLAY Phase:

1. Customized Solution
2. Maximizing Profit

The beautiful part of your products or services is that there are options for the Customer. In the **PLAY** Phase you are determining the right solution, but you are also trying to maximize your profits by aligning that Solution with the right pricing, terms, and terrific support and services (if applicable) to help maximize the effectiveness of the Solution for the Customer.

The best way to improve your success with the **PLAY** Phase is to seek counsel from your peers. While there may be some great training documents you can use, ultimately the best resource you will ever have is the people in the same role as you doing the same thing as you, but in a different territory. Peers training peers is always the more effective way to learn. Think of it this way—whom do you trust more, someone who teaches selling or someone who sells? And who do you trust more, someone who is great at selling or someone who is great at selling in your company? The point is, seek out best practices from your peers. Find out what mix worked best for them in similar situations.

CUSTOMIZED SOLUTION

In the Customer's mind, what you are selling is simply a product or service—just like all of the other products or services they have been pitched throughout the years. The Customer has you in a bucket, and they treat you the same way they treat everyone else. The sad truth is that in most sales scenarios they are right. There is no difference between the sales meetings they have been in lately. Salespeople focus on their company and their products. They talk about the amazing results you can achieve while using their products, and about the many others who have "seen the light" and bought their services.

You are different. You are a trusted advisor, and that is not how a trusted advisor would act. Would you give your friend advice on their life without first hearing them out? No way.

71

R-E-S-P-E-C-T.
Treat your Customers with the same consideration and respect you treat your friends, and you will become a trusted advisor.

The goal of the research and sales meetings is to develop a customized Solution for the Customer. One note here on "customized": we understand that you may not actually customize your products or services per account. The fact is, your product is what it is and there is no changing that. When we say customized, we are referring to positioning.

Any product can feel "customized" to meet my needs as a Customer if it is positioned properly. The way to do that is by explaining your product or service as a Solution — a Solution that fits them perfectly using the most powerful phrase in selling, "Based on what you've told me…"

Why is this the most powerful phrase in selling? Simple; it shows that the Solution you are presenting is what the Customer has asked for. You are using *their* words when presenting your Solution. For example, instead of saying that you have guaranteed on-time delivery within a 30-minute window, you would say, "remember how you said your time is very valuable and you get frustrated with your current provider delivering at all different times of the day? Well, your Solution will have guaranteed on-time delivery."

Hear the difference? One is presenting capabilities of the company and the other is presenting a Solution to a challenge uncovered in the Interview. The fact is, every Customer may get the guaranteed delivery because it's a standard practice for you. But when you position it as a feature of your company, it falls flat. When you position is it as an answer to their challenge, it is powerful.

At this point in the sale, though, you are concentrating your efforts on the Customer seeing value in the Solution you are considering for them (based on what they told you). *Benefits add value, whereas Features add cost.* The price of an item will ALWAYS be expensive or "too high" in the Customer's mind until they understand everything it will do for them. As they learn what the Solution will do for them, they start to see the value.

Remember that we are focusing on "What's In It For Me" with the benefit. Too many people get caught up in the "how it works" and not the "what it does for the Customer." Acting as an interpreter is part of your role here. Many times, the features are very technical and confusing. Explaining the "how it works" may not help at all. In fact, the more confused you make the Customer, the less likely they are to buy. Don't give them too much at one time. Space it out— make it a part of your overall conversation with them.

Always focus your benefits on the issues that stood out as important in the Interview. You can overload a Customer with too much information! Many salespeople feel that the more benefits they can stack up, the better their chances are of making the sale. This is not true at all. In fact, too many features can have the opposite effect. Remember the research of how many features a Customer actually uses or evaluates to make the buying decision? If you pummel them with features that are not related to specific things the Customer said in the Interview, then you are simply reducing your chances to close the sale. The price is going up and the value is going down.

THE PROPOSAL
Most of you reading this book will use some sort of formalized proposal. The **PLAY** Phase is where you will create your proposal to use in the next sales meeting. This is a solid practice and we are big fans of it. There is no better way to make the Solution feel "customized," than to see it laid out on paper in that form.

If you are like most companies, you bring in your slick glossy brochures that are pre-printed to use for the sales meeting. While these are valuable tools, there is no way to make the Solution feel customized to the Customer. You will be like every other salesperson coming in their office, and you can throw your trusted advisor status out the window.

Here are the top five things to remember when making your proposal:

1. **The front page should have the Customer's logo and not yours.** If the front page has your logo on it, you are giving them a document about you and not about them.

2. **Present compelling evidence of research.** Start with what you learned from the research and Interview. The second page in your proposal should be a recap of what you have learned.

3. **Use bullet points rather than paragraphs.** People do not like to read lengthy proposals. Plus, the more text it has, the more you are encouraging them to skip to the back and look at the price. Think of your proposal like your PowerPoint or Keynote presentations. You would never fill the slide with copy, you would always use bullet points. You would then add the color and detail.

4. **Show the business fit.** List the reasons (graphically) why your Company and theirs are a perfect fit together. (More on this later.)

5. **Make sure you have enough copies.** Yes, we have been in sales meetings where the salesperson only brought three copies of the proposal and there were eight people in the meeting. The hard copies of the proposal are for follow up. Try and meet with your soft copy where you are walking them through it. This takes courage, and is uncomfortable at first, but if you tell them they will get a copy of the presentation, then they are typically okay.

Once you have your proposal ready, it's time for the next sales meeting. If you are following our process, you already have the date and time set, so it's just the matter of delivery. Earlier, we mentioned that some sales cycles might require a demo, so we want to spend some time discussing demos and how to make them work for you. As you read through this next section, pay attention to the "Top Eight Demo Best Practices" list we share. These items apply not only to demos, but to the sales presentation as well. As you are presenting your proposal and preparing to ask for the order, use these techniques to guide your way to the ASK.

THE DEMO

For many of you, the demo of your product to the Customer is paramount to your closing the sale. A demo is a continuation of the conversation from the first meeting. While you may have done a quick demo of one feature just to "intrigue" them, this is when we will truly present the full demo as a *Solution* versus a product.

They are two parts to a demo strategy:
1. Demo
2. Evaluation

The difference is self-explanatory, but for proper definition: the **demo** is when *you* present the Solution to the Customer and the **evaluation** is when the *Customer* plays with it. Since sometimes it is very hard to make it an interactive demo, it is hard for the Customer to make the buying decision from the demo alone. It can happen, and if it does—fabulous! But since the percentages are against us in this area, the goal of the demo is often to get the Customer to do an evaluation of the Solution. The evaluation is when the Customer gets to use your Solution in their environment in a live setting. It gives them the chance to prove that what we have shown them is possible. Because getting to the evaluation requires a solid demo, let's focus our discussion on the demo.

The biggest mistake sales professionals make in demoing products to Customers is they present from *their* (the *salesperson's*) point of view, rather than the Customer's point of view. We tend to "sell" versus "demo," and there is a big difference.

DEMO VS. EVALUATION.
The demo is when you present the Solution to the Customer and the evaluation is when the Customer plays with it.

Selling is an art of connecting Customer goals, challenges, and needs to your Solutions. Demoing is the art of presenting our product as a Solution to the Customer's goals, challenges, or needs. Sounds the same, true, but the approach (and result) is very different.

Here are the **Top Eight Demo Best Practices:**

1. Be the Customer. Yes, it sounds odd, but if you want to be successful, you have to see the sale from your Customer's point of view, not your own. Let's illustrate with a story borrowed from the great book *Made to Stick: Why Some Ideas Survive and Others Die* by Chip and Dan Heath. [13]

In 1990, Elizabeth Newton earned a PhD in psychology at Stanford by studying a simple game in which she assigned people to one of two roles: "tappers" or "listeners." Tappers received a list of 25 well-known songs such as "Happy Birthday" and "The Star Spangled Banner." Each tapper was asked to pick a song and tap out the rhythm of the song to a listener by tapping on a table. The listener's job was to guess the song, based on the rhythm being tapped.

During the course of her experiment, the Listeners guessed the song only **2%** of time—but here is where it gets interesting. Before the listeners guessed the name of the song, the tappers had to predict the odds that the listeners would guess correctly. They predicted the odds at **50%**!

The tappers got their message across only **2%** of the time, but they thought they were getting their message across **50%** of the time! Why? When a tapper taps, they are hearing the song in their head. Meanwhile the listener can't hear that tune—all they can hear is a bunch of taps that sound like a messed up Morse code. In the experiment, the tappers are stunned at how hard it is for the listener to get the tune because the tune is so obvious to the tapper.

It is hard to be a tapper. The problem is, tappers have been given knowledge (the song title) that makes it impossible to imagine what it is like to lack that knowledge. Once we know something, we find it hard to imagine what it is like not to know it. It becomes difficult for us to share our knowledge with others.

We have used this illustration in hundreds of seminars and it always turns out the same (unless the people are cheating, which they often tend to do.)

The tapper/listener experiment is reenacted every day in sales demos everywhere. The tappers are the salespeople and the Customers are the listeners. We have grown so accustomed to working with our Solutions that all the features and benefits start to run together. We can throw them down faster than any Customer can pick them up. We assume the Customer "hears" the song we are playing. And, what Customer is going to tell you that they do not hear it?

CUSTOMER FEARS.
Remember, Customers do not want to look stupid in front of you to give you the "upper hand" in the sales process. They will play along and nod their head, but do they really, truly understand?

77

2. Do a customer demo, not a training session. To do this, only show the features (benefits) and functionality of the product or Solution you are demoing that directly relate to the information you received from the **PRESENT** Phase. That information came from time spent asking the right questions and understanding their goals, challenges, and needs. Your products have tons of features and functions built into them. They are robust and impressive, but they are only impressive to the Customer if they meet a goal or solve a problem the Customer actually has. Otherwise, it is just a chance for you to show off (and we all know that show-offs are not well-liked or well-received).

When demoing a function or feature, make it as quick and clean as possible. During a demo, there is no need to do the "deep dive" with a Customer—at least not on the first run through. If after you complete the demo, the Customer has a desire to go deeper, then go back and show them. But do not overload them during the initial pass of the demo.

DEMO SMART.

A good practice for demos is to ask the Customer what specific things they might like to see before you start. Use that to focus your demo.

Another great technique in this Phase is to be thinking to yourself, "What is the outcome the Customer wants to achieve?" When doing a demo, it's very easy to start talking about product features. This is one of the deadly sins of selling. As much as we want to talk about benefits to the Customer, for some reason we drift back to features. This is why keeping in mind the question, "what is the outcome the Customer is looking for?" can be very helpful.

3. Make it interactive. To do this, make sure that you check with the Customer for feedback frequently. Never assume they understand the benefit you are presenting—especially if you get all caught up in spewing features. You "assume" the Customer is tracking with you because, after all, this is their job. Perhaps they are tracking with the technical part of it, but are they connecting what you are demoing to the benefit for them? Do they see how this answers a challenge, solves a need, or helps them achieve one of their (or their company's) goals?

Never talk for more than 60 seconds without asking the Customer a question—even if it is just a simple tie-down. Don't look at the demo as if you were in the grammar school and it's show and tell. No, engage the Customer by asking questions. Remember, you don't know what they don't know and they know only what they want to know. Asking questions is the way to break this.

4. Connect the demo to the Customer. As we shared above, you never demo beyond what the Customer is looking for. During the demo, you get to use the most powerful phrase in selling, "Based on what you've told me." Always relate what you are demoing back to the **PRESENT** Phase, when you gathered the data from your Customer. Before you show a particular feature or function, set it up. For example say, "Remember how you told me you do not feel you have a theft problem in your company? Well, this report is known as the suspect devices report. It identifies devices in your system that may have left the building without you knowing. Let me show you how this works."

5. Listen. You will be amazed at what you can hear if you are focused on the Customer, instead of your demo. Too many people are so wrapped up in their demonstration that they are not really listening to what the Customer is saying. Listening helps you ascertain buying signals. For example, if they say, "This would be a good way to make sure we know what time everyone left the building at night," then they are telling you that your Solution is on the right track.

79

If they say, "I am not sure this is any better than what we have now," and you do not stop and deal with it at that moment, then you are about to spend a ton of time demonstrating a Solution they probably won't buy. At the very least, they have started to tune you out because they have already made the decision in their head that this will not work—so why pay any attention to anything else you are saying?

6. Do a demo, not a training class. Okay, this is similar number two, but it's important, so we are stressing the principle. Here is where we see more salespeople wander off the road than anywhere else. We have this incessant need to explain every option of every feature of every product. We try to answer every question we have ever been asked by other Customers as we are demoing to the Customer in front of us. For example, if you are a technology company, the key to great technology is that it is easy to use. If our demo takes 30 minutes for one feature, then suddenly your technology does not look so simple. While it is fair to say that it takes 30 minutes to cover every part of the feature, this is only true in training, not in demoing.

A demo of your product needs to be simple for the Customer to accept it. The tendency when demoing is to show all the options and variations in settings a Customer can do. During a demo, it is not the time to explain the four settings for each feature or explain how to do a custom setting for each one. In a demo, you simply point out that these options are there. Then, after you have completed the demo for this feature, you check for understanding and questions. If, and only if, the Customer asks for more detail, would you add it.

Customers are skeptical. They believe that all Solutions are hard. They believe that about every company's products. For example, they have bought before and been sold on how "easy" it was to use, yet when they went to implement it, they found a very different story. So, they are starting with the belief that it will be hard, and if the demo is cumbersome, then they just confirmed what they already believed about you to begin with!

7. Use Tie Downs. After you have demonstrated a benefit (feature), never move on until you have confirmation from the Customer that they have understood. Check to be sure that this is truly a value in their eyes. To do this, use a Tie Down. A Tie Down is a statement designed to gather agreement from the Customer. It is hung on the end of the sentence. For example, a company that can deliver at the same time every day is important to you, isn't it?

If what you have said represents truth as the Customer sees it, then they will respond by agreeing. And when they agree that the benefit you have just given meets their needs—they are moving closer to buying, aren't they?

Here are some more Tie Down examples you can use.

Aren't you…?
Don't you…?
Isn't it…?
Can't you…?
Didn't it…?
Won't you…?
Doesn't it…?
Wouldn't it…?

8. Everything Speaks. The Customer's words are only part of the story. Watching their non-verbal cues is just as important. Too many times, we are so into our demo that we are not paying attention to the cues our Customers are giving us. If they have doubts, you will notice them start to survey the other options available to them, such as their smartphone. At this point, they are not listening to you; they are tuned out. Never be afraid to stop your flow and check in with the Customer. Ask them if they understand. Ask them, "Do you see how this would benefit your business?" As explained in #4, connect the Customer to the demo. If you are demonstrating features they are not interested in, they will look to fill their minds with other things. Stay on track.

EVALUATIONS

The purpose of the demo is to get the Customer to buy the Solution, of course. But many times, the Customer needs the opportunity to "play" with your Solution. Truth be told, depending on how complicated your Solution is—even after a demo—the Customer probably still sees this as a product and not a Solution. So, giving them time to evaluate the Solution in their environment can be a key closing tool.

The objective is to get them to reveal "desired outcomes." You then fashion the solution against the needs. When you do the demo correctly, you will be able to explore the outcomes the Customer desires. Keep your mind focused on learning as much as you can about the Customer's desired outcomes. Keeping your focus on this solution will keep you from becoming obsessed with talking about your features.

MAXIMIZING PROFIT

This part of the **PLAY** Phase of Advisor Selling is the easiest to understand and comprehend. Simply put, you are trying to match the right price and delivery method for your Customer. Since you are selling a Solution and not a product, your "PLAY" should support this thought process. You should be able to say, "Based on what you've told me" when you present your PLAY for the Solution.

During this Phase, it is also the best time to introduce and include professional services or training for your Customer. If you package these offerings into the Solution versus separating them out, you will achieve two desired results. First, your Customer will be able to exceed their expectations of the Solution because they will be better trained and better equipped to take full advantage of it. And secondly, your sale will stay sold.

SELLING SERVICE.
Don't wait till after they make the buying decision to introduce your professional services. By then, it's often times too late.

We do a lot of work with retailers. One thing we notice is that when they buy a new point of sale system, they usually opt out of any training or services because the price is so high. The net result is they have a glorified cash register since they have no clue how to work 80% of the features of that POS system. It's natural for a Customer paying thousands of dollars for your solution to expect that they should not have to pay for professional services on top of that. In fact, we feel the same way when we buy something. But the point here is not about something being broken; it's about helping the Customer get the most value from your solution.

It's always been ironic to me that Apple gets such high praise for creating the genius bar in its stores when in fact, the reason no one used to buy Apple products was because no one knew how to work them! If people were intimidated by how to operate an Apple, then was the genius bar a stroke of genius or was it marketing to sell products?

If you've followed the Advisor Selling process thus far, when you present services, they will be seen as part of the Solution, and not as the extras your Customer has to buy to be able to do business. I remember when Lexus first came to the States, I was very intrigued by this new level of luxury car. I wanted to go experience it for myself. The first thing the salesman did was take me to the service area and show me their 14-bay department. He bragged about how you could eat off the floors because they were so clean. I was very impressed, of course, but it wasn't until the drive home that I realize I'm going to spend that much money for a car the last thing I think I will need is service. But that's not what the salesman was trying to tell me. He wanted me to know that even though they built the best car in the world, if there was ever a need for service, they also had the best service in the world.

PRICING

Price is not a sustainable competitive advantage. Don't think for a moment you're going to be able to build a business based on being the cheapest. There will always be somebody somewhere who will be able to make, produce, ship, design, or provide what you're offering a little cheaper. In the 1960s, if you wanted the best price on something, you went to Sears. In the 1970s and 1980s, Sears was replaced by K-Mart. By the time the 1990s arrived, it was Wal-Mart with the cheapest price. And now we're watching Amazon overtake Wal-Mart as the lowest price provider. Price may allow you to win today, but it will never allow you to win for an extended period of time.

Using price as the reason you're superior completely eliminates the role you play in the sales process and is admitting what you have is merely a commodity. Regardless of what you sell and the number of competitors you may have, you cannot view what you have as a commodity.

The objective of the sales process is to uncover Customer needs that allow you to fashion your Solution to **not** be focused on price. Price should not be a key reason why a Customer buys from you.

We are not saying price is to be ignored. What we are saying is your ability to close a sale must be on the merits of how you are going to help the Customer.

Remember, this is Advisor Selling, not "Selling Cheap." The most beautiful outcome of "Advisor Selling" is the ability to be the best value to the Customer because of how you are able to meet their needs or desired outcomes.

One reason salespeople have problems with price, is they invite trouble right from the start. If a salesperson can't deliver their price with confidence, then why should a Customer accept it?

A VP of purchasing for a major company shared with me one time how he instructs all of his buyers to study the body language and confidence of every salesperson they meet. Specifically, he instructed his salespeople to always push back on price if the salesperson showed even the slightest hesitation in either speech or body language when discussing price. His rationale was simple. If the salesperson had any doubts about price, it would show in their body language, and his buyers could then extract a discount. What is sad about this is the strategy was used regardless if the buyer thought the price was too high or not. It didn't matter. If they felt they could get a lower price, they would go for it.

Price must be presented with strong body language and no hesitation in voice, followed by silence. The worst thing a salesperson can do is present a price and then immediately follow it with something lame like, "I'm sure we can figure out something that will work for you." Forget it! Saying that or anything similar to that is only inviting the Customer to demand a discount. You state your price with confidence and then be silent. If after a bit the Customer doesn't say anything, then follow it with a statement that closes the sale—something like, "Let's go ahead and set up the PO. What day would you like us to start?" In this manner, what you're doing is closing the sale without inviting discussion.

Keep in mind, businesses don't *buy* anything. They only invest. They invest because they need something that is going to help them achieve their objectives. What this means is Customers will pay an amount equal to or less than the value they expect to receive from the products or services you're selling.

An example might be a new computer system. A Customer may have two options—one costing $200,000 and the other $600,000. Looking at the two amounts, someone would naturally assume the $200,000 option is the best price. However, it may be a far more expensive option if it doesn't deliver on what the Customer wants.

AN OBJECTION IS A QUESTION.
When a Customer objects, it means they need more information. It does not mean lower your price.

When a Customer objects to your price, what they're saying is they do not see enough value in what you're selling to be worth the price they're being asked to pay. This is one reason why price should never be discussed until you are well into the selling process and have been able to uncover the Customer's critical needs and desires.

When the Customer does bring up price before you have a good handle on their needs, you need to be upfront with the Customer and say something like, "We have a number of different solutions and I'm not sure which one would be right for you, so it would be premature to discuss price until I know more about your needs." However you phrase it, the result is the same. You don't want to give them a price until you know their needs.

A key reason why it's important to know the Customer's needs before you give them a price is it gives you leverage when you do give them a price. If the Customer objects to your price, the response you give should be a question regarding one of the Customer's key needs. Let's walk through an example as to how this might look during a sales call.

> **Customer:** I like your ideas, but your price is simply too high.

> **Salesperson:** You shared how you need to have the new equipment in place and running in five weeks. What is the risk to your business if that doesn't happen?

Customer: If we don't have the equipment running in five weeks, then we won't be able to meet the requirements of the new contract we have.

Salesperson: What you're saying is having everything in place in five weeks or less is essential, right?

Customer: Yes. I don't even want to think about what could happen if we didn't make that date.

Salesperson: Good. That's why we need to get going with the project today so you don't have to worry. Let's get a PO set up.

What you've done is taken the price and made it a secondary issue to the critical needs they have.

As successful as this approach is, there are times when it still won't work. The key through the entire discussion regarding price is to not allow yourself to be in a situation where cutting your price becomes the focal point of your strategy.

Providing the Customer with options is many times a great way to ensure price is not an issue. At the same, this allows you to demonstrate to the Customer the value of who you are.

The best way to provide options is by giving the Customer three different plans from which they can pick. This does not mean it's a buffet where people can pick and choose. No, what this means is you provide the Customer with three distinct options. Each one has the ability to stand on its own.

The way you present "option pricing" is by first presenting your highest price option. This does two things. First, it allows you to show the Customer everything you could offer. Second, by providing the Customer with the most expensive option as the first one, it allows them to become price conditioned. This means when you present the second option that is priced lower, it will be more appealing if they are price-oriented in their thinking.

With the second option, it is important the package still be a complete offering from which the Customer will benefit. To complete the process, you can then present a third option that is even lower in price. With this third option, the offering must be very limited in how it will benefit the Customer. Objective is the lowest-price option is so limiting in nature that it makes either the first or second the only ones they see as options.

The benefit of using this "option pricing" is that it allows the Customer to feel like they are in control, because they are the one deciding which option to buy. The second benefit is it allows the Customer to see the full array of options. Many times, that alone generates even more discussion, which often can lead to even another sale.

Regardless of the approach you use, do not allow the Customer to dictate pricing. Confidence in the communication process is going to do more than almost anything else in helping to minimize the need for negotiation.

SELL FIRST.
The best way to avoid negotiating is by selling first.

A great concept to remember is, "Sell first. Negotiate second." What this means is focus your effort on selling, and in particular using the "Advisor Selling" concept. When you do this, the effort is on uncovering the needs of the Customer and positioning your offer as being the best solution to solve their needs.

A good track to follow is to never allow yourself to enter into any negotiations with a Customer until they've rejected your offer at least twice.

Watch how this can play out. My phone rang one morning and it was a prominent businessperson who had a very senior level position in a company. He began the conversation by immediately asking me what my fee was. Despite the person being someone I respected, I held back and responded by asking him questions about his needs. After a 10-minute telephone discussion where I got him to share with me what his needs were, I provided him with my price. After a moment of silence, he responded with a comment about how it seemed quite high and there was no way he could agree to it. My response was, "That's fine. Feel free to call me if you change your mind." The conversation quickly ended.

Being the salesperson I am, I made notes on the call and put a note into my calendar to call the person back in two days. I never made that call. The next day the businessperson called me back and informed me how he had met with the CEO and they agreed they needed to bring me in at the full fee. The lesson learned? Be patient, state your price, and allow the Customer to reject it.

The best criteria you can use for determining if you should negotiate with a Customer is to make sure you have answers to the following questions:

★ Has the Customer rejected my offer at least twice?

★ Do I know at least two critical needs the Customer has that I can help them with?

★ Do I know when they intend to make a decision?

★ Do I know for sure that I'm dealing with the decision maker?

If you don't have the answers to each of these questions, don't allow yourself to begin negotiating. The reason is simple—you'll lose!

Never view negotiating as a game of seeing how much one person can take from another. View negotiating as a process of helping the Customer achieve success in dealing with the needs they have.

DELIVERY

Here we are examining the Customer's preferred method of delivery for your services. For example, do they buy directly or through an expediter? Many government agencies require you work through an intermediary. Whatever process the Customer follows, it is up to you to match it and not try to convince them to use your system.

In this Phase, you are also outlining payment terms, payment options, etc. For example, do you need some milestones in the process for payment? If you are selling services, this may be you. Your Customer may require the work to be done before they pay, but are willing to make a deposit and will fund the project based on hitting certain milestones.

It's also important to understand the Customer's budgeting process. Your delivery of goods and services needs to align with when they have funding available. Most companies today have a strict budgeting process. You may hear the objection "I love it, but I have to wait until the next budget cycle."

In this case, try splitting the project or payment over the budget cycles. We lost a deal one time because the Customer said they had no budget for it. We were 60 days from the next annual budget—in which they got another $250,000 for our type of project. Had we been smart enough to align with their delivery method, we could have won that deal. In fact, we found out later that the reason we lost was that the other company offered to split the billing between the two budget years. They even made it two separate projects to help the Customer not call attention to the fact they were splitting the money between fiscal years. The good news for you is that this lesson only cost you the price of this book.

SEVEN

ASK PHASE

After you have determined the best **PLAY**, you are ready to move on to the next Phase—the **ASK**. In other words, you have done your homework. You have created the perfect Solution for the Customer—based on what they told you—and now it is time to AFTO—Ask for the Order! (Yes, we are old school when old school works.)

There are two steps in the ASK Phase:

1. **Business Fit**
2. **AFTO (Ask for the Order)**

The foundation of these two steps is built around confidence. The Customer is looking to have confidence in you, the salesperson, and your company. At the same time, you must have confidence in yourself. Confidence sells. It comes down to a basic belief that your level of confidence and competence is going to determine your level of success.

The info in this next section applies to your proposal and how you design it for this sales meeting. So, as you read, think not only about the way you will deliver this message in the sales meeting, but also how you would craft or frame your written proposal as well. Keep in mind the purpose of Business Fit is to setup the close. The better job you do with Business Fit, the more likely you are to get a 'yes' when you AFTO.

BUSINESS FIT

Most salespeople underestimate the significance of Business Fit. They assume that the only concern for a Customer is either price, technology, or product specs. In fact, today's Customer is just as interested in you and your company being the right "fit" to provide the Solution, as they are the product's capabilities.

You are not the only Solution out there. You are not the cheapest Solution out there. (If you are the cheapest, Advisor Selling may not be for you.) But, you are the best—at least you believe so (and that is not an ego thing, but a confidence one). Before you ask for the order, though, first you must present your case.

Business fit has two components:

1. Company alignment
2. Solution alignment

Company alignment is when you draw the comparisons between their company and yours. Talk about your shared values, common purpose in service, or passion for a particular cause that you both support.

For example, when we were working with a technology company that sold a SaaS service for protecting mobile devices in the workplace, we encouraged them to focus on the shared value of security or the common purpose of device management. In another case, we were working with a recycling company. There, we emphasized the core value of sustainability shared between the two companies. We were saying, "if your company believes in sustainability, then there is no more innovative or passionate company about sustainability than us. However, if you just see recycling as another from of trash, then we are not the right fit for you."

The corporate profile, organizational structure, key players, and political map all contribute to the Business Fit, which Mark Shonka defines in his book *Beyond Selling Value* as: "how two companies, working together, can help the Customer achieve critical objectives, implement important strategies, and address important issues. While the business fit will be different for every account, it always identifies the basis for a long-term, strategic relationship, and states the value of the relationship in the Customer's terms. Thus, it typically focuses on the business priorities of senior management." [14]

For a service company, you want to connect the core value proposition of the Customer to your core value prop. For example, let's say that the Customer has a mission statement on their website that says "making life easier for our clients." Then you should show how your Solution will make life easier for the Customer and in so doing will make *their* Customer's lives easier. See the connection—or should we say "fit"? Never assume a Customer or prospect sees the business fit on their own—it rarely happens that way.

For a technology company, Solution alignment is often times referred to as "technical fit." Technical fit, as it sounds, is how the technology will fit the company's needs. Is it a good fit? Is it a complicated fit? Remember not to fall into the Customer trap of letting business fit turn into a technology discussion. Focus the conversation on how your Solution fits and not how your technology fits. This may seem counterintuitive in a high-tech IT environment, but it does work.

For a manufacturing company, their core value is often quality or efficiency. If its quality, then use proof sources from other Customers to show how you have delivered quality over the years. Or, show your company's commitment to quality through the number of hours of training of quality training that all of your employees go through each year. It is powerful to hear stats that show how your company achieves its level of quality, rather than saying "quality is one of our core values." And to take it one step further, find a proof source on yourself as the sales professional.

BUSINESS FIT IS ABOUT ALIGNMENT.
Customers care as much about you, your company and your ability to deliver on the promise as they do about your products or services (Solution).

Recently, I had a call with a potential client about a consulting project with their organization. They were impressed with my answers and for next steps; they wanted me to write a paper on what life would be like working with me. Since the person I was dealing with had a background in HR, I used a subtle form of Business Fit and said, "I would be happy to write you a paper, but that is a lot like someone writing a resume for a job opening. Ultimately, it is the answers to the interview questions and examples of behavior in similar situations that matter, isn't it?" (Catch the tie-down?)

After getting positive confirmation, I continued, "Don't you think it would be better for you to speak to someone I have worked for in the past that had a similar situation to hear what they have to say?" The point here is that to demonstrate my Business Fit, I used a proof source—a reference from someone outside of the conversation. An unbiased source who has no stake in the decision. Obviously, we have to be very good at our job to get someone to give up 30 minutes of his or her time for a reference call. But, if we are practicing Advisor Selling and we have achieved trusted advisor status, you will be amazed at how simple this request is to make.

But the most important part of Business Fit is to go deep. Don't simply put their list of core values on the left side of the slide and your company's core values on the right to show how similar they are. This might be a good technique, but for most people, they have no idea what the core values of their company actually are. So they don't light up when you do this.

Rather, in your analysis of their business, think about what you learned about how they go about their day-to-day routine. For example, we once worked with a company that had just gone through a process improvement initiative (TQM). As we spoke with people, we constantly heard terms like "team" and "engineer." So when we presented our Solution, we made sure to mimic that language. We showed them how we work in teams and how our process required members of the Customer's company to be on our team for "engineering" any process.

We spoke of the value we shared by saying "we never engineer a solution until we have spent time inside the organization to learn the current state." It was amazing how using their terms and language in the appropriate way resonated with the Customer. In fact, we never had to Ask for the Order, the Solution pitch (ASK) rolled into a conversation of who needed to be on the team. The next thing you know, we were putting together a timeline for roll out—and we never got to the price slide! (I wish it happened that way every time.)

Naturally, we are going to share a story of the "perfect" example. But truthfully, we cannot stress the importance of Business Fit enough. It not only helps in the buying decision, but later as we talk about turning your Customer into an evangelist for you, you will see how arming them with Business Fit will help protect your place in their annual budget.

BEST SALE EVER.
The best sale is a sale that leads to the next one.

One word of caution around Business Fit—focus on tangibles, not on ideals. Too many salespeople will focus on ideal situations and not on the tangible things that both companies can commit to and deliver on—and don't make this exercise trite. We've been in sales meetings where the salesperson tried to deliver Business Fit and it sounded a little condescending. The connections she was drawing was so generic that they could apply to any company. It would be like choosing a mate for life based on the fact that you like grapes and they like grapes, you like sports and they like sports, or you like the Cowboys and they like the Cowboys.

Make sure that each time you list a Business Fit, you also explain *how* it is a Business Fit. The Business Fit may not be an identical fact about each company, but identical *traits* about each company. For example, you might list commitment to excellence as one of your Business Fit ideas. You do not say you're committed to excellence and we're committed to excellence—that, again, sounds trite. Instead, give them a specific example that demonstrates your commitment to excellence and compare it to an example of the Customer's commitment to excellence.

One time, we were on a sales call and the Business Fit example was the shared value of highly trained passionate people in each company. The reference was the fact that the company ranked in the Top 100 Places to Work in America.

After you have demonstrated the Business Fit, you are ready to close and ask for the order (AFTO).

AFTO

The most frequent part left out of a sales presentation is the close. Salespeople are hesitant to try and close the sale due to their own lack of confidence. Throughout this book, we have been demonstrating how to ensure you have confidence by following each of the steps we've laid out. Sales is a process. Follow the process and it will take you to a natural close.

It was a perfect day to close sales, or at least I thought it was with one particular salesperson I remember working with. He had great communication skills and an amazing ability to ask questions and to develop a great solution for the Customer. It was 8:45 AM and I was listening to what I feel is one of the sharpest salespeople I've ever been around. I'm thinking to myself "what could I possibly teach this guy, and why did his manager want me to work with him."

The call was going great and I was anxious to see what type of closing technique he was going to use with the Customer. In my mind I was thinking this is a slam-dunk. The Customer sees the value and has a definite need. It was at that point I almost fell out of my chair. The salesperson that had seemed so brilliant moments earlier, closes the sale by stating the following: "It's been great talking with you. Here's the customer service phone number; when you want to place an order, just go ahead and call them." And with that, he thanked the Customer and walked out the door.

No need to ask if I was ready to blow a gasket. I was and I didn't waste any time. Once we were in the parking lot, I began asking him what happened in there. The salesperson looked at me in shock, he felt great. His comment to me was "that was a great call, hopefully we will have more like that today." Excuse me, but I'm flipping out in amazement at how he thought it was a great call.

Immediately, I asked him about how he asked for the order and again, he said that was how he closed every call. I challenged him and after five minutes of dancing around, he explained to me that this was the only closing technique he was comfortable using because he was so afraid the Customer might say "no." He went on to explain how after he began using that approach, he was much more relaxed and could, therefore, focus on the selling process and really listen to the Customer.

If you're wondering how he was able to correct his inability to close, I'll tell you, he wasn't; and he soon found himself out of a job. The core of his problem was that he never came to realize how he was able to help his Customers. This prevented him from ever having enough confidence in himself to be able to close the deal for fear of potentially facing rejection.

Becoming a successful closer requires three things. First, you need to have confidence to know that what you're doing is going to make a difference. Second, you must have confidence in yourself and your sales process. Third, you need to know how you're going to close the sale before you get there. Mastering those three things will increase your closing ratio and, in turn, the number of Customers you're able to help.

Too many times, we have been on sales calls that ended like that last story. It always amazes me that salespeople go all the way through the process and sit back and say "ta-da!" and wait for the Customer to be so awe-inspired that they cannot help but whip out their pen and sign the contract immediately. I'm not sure what sales training they went to, or what movies they have been watching, but it never happens like this in real life. Customers expect you to close. It is respectful. It is your responsibility. If you leave it up to the Customer, they WILL NOT CLOSE! (Hard to believe we have to write that, but after 25 years and over 1,000 ride alongs, all evidence points to that need.)

AFTO

It is your responsibility to ask for the sale. You must close. NEVER wait on the Customer to do it for you—they rarely will.

Here is the really sad part of selling. We wrote an article last year ti-tled "The biggest crime in selling" that got a lot of pickup around the world. It essentially said this—in selling, the Customer will close for you enough times that you can survive and make a living. If we only paid commission on the deals where salespeople actually asked for the order, then you could not earn a living. The crime, as we stated, was that people are in sales, and surviving, because they get lucky enough to meet Customers who AFTO themselves—and they never have to! Nothing is more upsetting to a hard-working sales professional than seeing a non-selling salesperson fall into a big, high-paying deal. It's just not fair. We agree that as soon as we figure out a way to only pay commission to the sales professionals and not the clerks, we will let you know.

In order to properly ask the Customer to buy, key phrasing is nec-essary. Close-ended statements that elicit a specific response are great ways of determining if the sale is completed. If you think about it, when you use the Advisor Selling process—meaning you did a thorough interview in the **PRESENT** Phase to determine their goals, challenges, and needs, and then crafted a Solution that really answers all of these in the **PLAY** Phase, then the next step is a logical one, isn't it? You ASK FOR THE ORDER! (Okay, I think we have made our point.)

To do this, we assume the sale and use the following phrase. "Since we've agreed." This phrase is the starting point for you. It connects to the rest of the process by setting up the fact that what you have presented is what they need to reach their goals, solve their problem, or fill their needs.

After the phrase "since we've agreed," you simply relate the benefits of the Solution in a quick list and then finish with a simple phrase like: "what date would you like to start the install?" Or, "would you like me to make sure this Solution gets added to your next PO?" Or even more direct like, "I checked with the warehouse before coming over, and we set the date for your service to start Thursday; is that soon enough?"

For example, you might say:

> *Since we've agreed that our Solution allows you to see all your devices in one console (which you said was important to you), allows you to deploy patches and updates to your devices remotely (which you said was a challenge for you now), and allows you to manage the power usage of all of the devices on the network, reducing your energy spend (which is one of your goals for this year), what are the next steps to get this installed?*

Notice how in the example, we started with the assumptive agreement phrase and then listed three quick benefits that relate to their goals, challenges, and needs, and *then* asked for the order.

Or, let's say you're a printing company selling printing services. You might AFTO by saying:

> *Since we've agreed that the document solution we have customized for you allows all of your employees to print from their devices, versus having to leave their desk to print (which was important to you), and it collates and staples documents so that they're ready when they pick them up, saving time and money on payroll, I've got you scheduled to start service on Thursday. Is it best for us to come by in the morning or in the afternoon?*

In the last example, you read how the salesperson called out some specific parts of the Solution that came from the Interview and related the benefit that goes along with that Solution. Instead of asking, "what do you think? Would you like to try us?", the salesman assumed the sale and gave a specific date for start of service. When you use this technique, the Customer's response is about the delivery date not about whether they want your product or service. If you use an assumptive close process, there is no decision to be made whether or not to buy; the decision is simply when to start.

There are many ways to Ask for the Order. And if you have become skilled at this, then use your method. Please do not read this as if the only way to close a sale. What we're representing here is the best way to close a sale in a solution selling process.

IT'S THEIR SOLUTION.
Advisor Selling done right will put you into a position to use the simple phrase "since we've agreed."

When working with salespeople, I'm frequently asked what closing technique I use—it's simple. I use the one described above, the assumptive approach. I use it for two reasons; first, I always expect the Customer to buy, and second, I've used the techniques laid out in this book, so I fully understand that it makes sense for the Customer to buy from me and to buy now.

Use the needs and desires the Customer has told you to guide you to your close. No need to make it any harder than you have to. This is what makes the demo portion of the sales call so beneficial. The Customer should have revealed valuable information when you were using the eight best practices. The better the level of discussion during the demo, the easier it will be to close the sale. Optimizing the Advisor Selling process means the close is built on allowing the Customer to achieve success with the two biggest needs or desired outcomes they have. Don't attempt to build a solution that allows the Customer to achieve everything. Rarely is that approach going to be successful. This is because Customers become skeptical of salespeople who view the products or services they have to sell as being the perfect solution to everything. There's no need to make things difficult by giving the Customer doubt. Keeping your solution focused on a couple of needs allows you to avoid that trap.

Lastly, when you use an assumptive close, you are linked to and aligned with the most powerful phrase in selling, "based on what you've told me." The entire Solution you crafted for them is based on what they told you. So, it makes sense that if you have given them what they want (based on what they told you), the logical conclusion is "since we've agreed" when you ask for the order.

Because Advisor Selling's consultative sales approach is the best way to make the sale while becoming a trusted advisor, Customers will always say yes when you AFTO, right? You might want to read on.

EIGHT

ANSWER PHASE

It would be awesome if we could design a sales process that did not require this Phase, but, truth be told, even if the Customer is thoroughly impressed with you and your Solutions, they will still probably object—maybe not to the product, but to making the buying decision. Be prepared, even if they love everything about you and the Solution, their natural instinct is to object—so they will!

If you follow all of the Phases and steps in this sales process just as we have prescribed, you honestly have answered the vast majority of objections the Customer might have. In fact, most times when they object, it's because you missed something along the way, or did not follow the process correctly.

It never ceases to amaze us the number of times a Customer objects, even with our sales process. You see, it's often not a failure of the process, rather a success of it. Customers are so amazed by the Solution you are presenting and how it truly fits their wants, interests, needs, and desires and helps them achieve their goals or solve a problem, that they are a bit caught off guard. A confident Customer will smile, shake your hand, and tell you how much they appreciate you. A less than confident Customer will object—not because they truly have an objection, but more because they are so used to always objecting at this point; it's just habit.

Whatever the reason for the objection, they do occur. And we certainly would have no credibility if we said that they did not or that the presence of the objection was a reflection on your failure in the process. Rather, lets just say that objections are a reality, a necessary evil of the sales process. We will not try to sugarcoat and say that objections are good news, but we do believe that they are a good sign, and not something to be bothered by.

There are two parts to the ANSWER Phase:

1. Objections
2. AFTO (yes again)

OBJECTIONS

Objections are really nothing more than *questions* — thus the name of this Phase. Think back to a time when you were making a significant purchase. Did you have objections? Why? How did you feel? If you liked everything about the item, why did you hesitate? Do you think it's possible that you tried to talk yourself out of the purchase? What do you think made you feel this way? Was it really an objection, or just more of a question?

When the Customer objects, he is waiting on you to ask him to buy. We cannot stress this point enough. The Customer wants to be shown why they need to buy. After all, this is a major decision that is not only about money, but also about how it will impact their work lives over the next few years and how it will help them engage the rest of the company. In may cases, this buying decision can impact his or her future mobility within the company, so its very important to them on many levels, which is why we stressed Business Fit in the last Phase.

There is another way to think about objections, though. When you want something, it's human nature to come up with a reason why you can't have it. Take, for example, the most common objection: "It's too expensive." Every time you've treated yourself to a luxury, hasn't the thought "it's too expensive" run through your mind? In fact, isn't the fact that "it's too expensive" part of the reason you want it in the first place?

Most, if not all, sales objections contain the seeds of a successful sale. "I want to think it over" implies that the Customer actually wants to buy. Even the "I've heard your support is not good" has the hidden message that "if it weren't for that, I'd be buying." Tom Hopkins, arguably the dean of sales trainers, puts it this way: "Until you hear an objection, you're not going to make a sale." [15]

So there's no reason to lose heart when the inevitable objections surface. The challenge is what to do about them.

IT'S NOT PERSONAL.
IT'S JUST BUSINESS.
Remember, objections are merely questions—they are not attacks against you.

You must see things from the Customer's point of view, and have a positive mental attitude toward the objection. If you were a Customer (or Customer somewhere else) and raised objections, and a "salesperson" quickly dismissed them, how would you feel? Not good, right? And I am sure you don't want one of your Customers to feel that same way, do you? (Nice use of a tie-down, wasn't it?)

Answering objections is a three-part process. You:

1. Soften
2. Ask
3. Answer

SOFTEN

Softening phrases are phrases we use to let the Customer know we understand their concerns and that they have a right to be concerned. It is up to us to make them feel confident and comfortable with their buying decision. We don't want to sound pushy, so we use softening phrases to show the Customer that we appreciate their point of view.

If we act like an objection is unusual for us, then our confidence meter goes way down and the Customer sees it. I had an old coach that used to say, "Act like you have been there before." If your first reaction is to say something like, "but in the last conversation, you said price was not an issue, and now you are saying it is." You might as well hang it up.

Softening the objection is a form of sales confidence. It shows patience and no fear or panic on your part. It's also very disarming for the Customer. They are not used to someone agreeing with him or her when they object. Here are some good softening phrases you can use:

Good Softening Phrases

> *I understand how you feel.*

> *I'm not surprised to hear you say that.*

> *A lot of my Customers say the same thing.*

> *You've brought up a good point.*

> *I can understand your concern.*

It's also a good practice to put the stated objection together with the softening phrase. For example:

> *I understand how you feel. After all, you will have to live with this decision for a very long time, and the last deployment you made had tons of issues.*

Or:

> *I'm not surprised to hear you say that. After all, you have been with your current provider for over XX years now, and this is a big change not only for your company, but for you, as well.*

The softening phase is what makes this technique work. At this point, most salespeople will dive into 12 verses of "why their product is the perfect product." But instead, you *soften* their objection and, in essence, let them know it's okay to object in the first place.

We have seen many, many sales lost at this point in the process, because the salesperson develops verbal diarrhea and reverts back to their old selling methods. Sadly, we've even been on some sales calls where the salesperson loved this part of the sale. It was a game to them—a conquest. And while you may feel great as the guy standing at the end of the fight, you will not become a trusted advisor.

A trusted advisor listens to and empathizes with his or her Customer's situation. She softens the objection and lets the Customer know it's okay feel the way he is feeling right now, and that there is no big battle.

ASK

So, what are you doing when you "Ask," the second part of answering objections? You are determining exactly what it is that concerns the Customer. Often when someone objects, the reason they give is not truly the question they are wrestling to make this decision.

Never assume you know the answer to an objection. You must first check for understanding, and then answer. Most times, the true "objection" is not coming out—the Customer is simply using a line they have become accustomed to as a way of avoiding saying yes to your close. Customers will use a line that has worked many times on weaker salespeople, but not you!

For example, the Customer might object by saying, "I'm not sure we can afford this right now." If you've done your research properly, you probably know that this doesn't make sense. After all, why would you be trying to close a sale that they could not afford?

So, when they do object, you need to get to the bottom of it, or in other words, get to the "real" objection. You might say something like:

> *I understand your concern, after all this is an investment by your company and you want to make sure it is a good one. But, based on what you've told me, this Solution perfectly fits what you have been searching for, so is affordability your concern, or is there something else bothering you?*

While this is a generic example, as you can predict, the answer to the question will flush out the true objection—which is the purpose of this tool. Since this is a question, feel free to use the word "question." For example, say something like "is the question in your mind…" or "what is the question you're trying to answer now?" Using the word "question" actually helps to put the Customer at ease, and lets them know that this is not a confrontation, but a dialogue.

ANSWER

After you have Softened and Asked, it is time to Answer. Here is where you get to use the most powerful phrase in selling again (you can never use this phrase too much, by the way). Always start by affirming your Customer. Say something like, "okay, I understand your concern. But based on what you've told me…" and then answer their objection. Yes, it is that simple.

The best answers always refer back to the original Interview with the Customer where you discovered their goals, challenges, and needs. Try not to "sell" here. You are not presenting your Solution all over again; you are simply connecting the "fit" to the question (objection). You can also use a phrase here like, "remember when we were in the paint department, and you told me about the mistakes that happen in product labels?" Here, we are not only referring back to the Solution, but also back to the research we put into this Solution.

NEVER ARGUE.
You enter into an argument when you use your words. You enter into a debate when you use theirs.

There are multiple tools to use when trying to answer an objection. The one described above is considered to be the best, since its main purpose is not only to answer the objection, but also to drill down into the *true* objection. Remember, we are not trying to replace the clubs in your golf bag; we are trying to add to them.

An alternate approach for dealing with questions raised by the Customer is using the same "Soften, Ask, Answer" approach as described above, but this time, ask a question of clarification tied to one of the Customer's key goals or desired outcomes. This approach is designed to get the Customer thinking about the big picture, which is their needs.

Many times, getting the Customer to focus on their needs will get them to realize that, although they may have a question, the bigger concern in their mind is solving their need.

After you have answered their objection, do you need to ask for the order again? Do bears bare? Do bees be? Of course, you do! You must remember that once you feel confident you have answered the Customer's objection, you must, once again, ask the Customer to buy. You can use phrases similar to those used when asking the Customer to buy the first time.

It is your job to ask for the order. Customers expect you to do so. You must be confident and assertive. Use the techniques you learned in the last Phase. And when you do, they will say "yes" and you can move on to the **ADVISE** Phase.

NEGOTIATING

Up to now we've talked exclusively about the selling process, and little about negotiation and the role it has in sales. The reason is simple—you can't negotiate anything until you've, first, sold. One of the biggest problems salespeople have is thinking the only way to close a sale is by negotiating.

One morning, while I was preparing to conduct an account manager workshop for a major company, a salesperson approached me and asked, "Negotiating is one of the best ways to close the sale, right?" I was taken aback by the question, because I could tell by his voice that he wanted me to say that it wasn't just one of the best ways, but it was the absolute very best way. There was no way I was going to tell him that.

Here's what I told him: "Maybe, but it will come with a hefty destruction of profit. Too many salespeople are negotiating when they really should be selling. Are you one of them? If so, it's costing you and your company dearly."

Needless to say, this wasn't what he was hoping to hear. Now, just so you don't think my goal was to run him over with a bus, let me explain more. My goal was to get him thinking. I explained to him that his question was excellent, and it was at the heart of what we would be addressing in the training.

You should never feel that the only way to close a sale is by negotiation. One way to avoid negotiating all together is to sell first, negotiate second. When you sell first—and genuinely uncover the true needs of the Customer—you will rarely have a need for negotiation.

You will be able to match your benefits to the Customer, and the Customer will see that you are not asking too much with your full price offer. Every page of the book, up to now, has been written to give you the tools and the confidence you need to be able to uncover the Customer's needs.

Some of you are probably asking, *"But what if I can't close the sale without offering a discount?!"* Our response? It's probably not a sale worth having.

If your mind isn't confused enough, let us add that we believe many companies should introduce a "no negotiation" policy. Too often, profit is compromised when the salesperson has the green light to adjust pricing on the spot, without having to secure approval from anyone else. The problem is, if salespeople have authority to negotiate under any circumstance, they will lean toward negotiation that sabotages profit. Sure, they don't go into it thinking this, but trust me—the negotiating typically leads straight to a path of offering a discount. The "no negotiation" policy can—and will—work.

Now that you're questioning the idea of no negotiation on price, let us add that this does not mean you can't negotiate. You can still negotiate—you're just negotiating on things other than price. Stop and ask yourself about all of the things you offer that go beyond price. Your list should be quite long. If it's not, then you don't know what you're selling, and you don't know your Customer. The key thing to remember is, negotiating does not have to always be about price.

Negotiate over things that won't kill profit. In other words, offering a discount on price should rarely, if ever, be used. You can negotiate by making concessions that are not strictly price-based, such as bumping up service slightly, offering more favorable delivery times, and so forth.

THE TRUTH ABOUT PRICE.
A sale at a reduced price is not better than no sale at all.

Sometimes, the wisest decision you can make is to not budge on price and instead stay focused on the Customers who are the best fit for what you offer—and are willing to pay for it. You begin to see that having a policy of not negotiating on price isn't so outlandish at all. We can tell you from experience—companies that have put the "no negotiation" policy in place have found themselves initially struggling with major complaining from salespeople. However, in every case, once the initial complaining subsides and the sales team knows they're not going to get control of pricing again, they move on and focus on Customer outcomes. The result? Their attention on selling increases, and they close sales that are far more profitable. In other words, they are Maximizing Profits (a step in the **PLAY** Phase.)

I bet you're wondering if this strategy precludes any ability to flex on price. No; as the sales manager, or someone at least one step removed from the sales process, is the one who controls any changes to pricing. By having it one step removed, though, it takes away all quick tendencies to cut prices.

Just because we're talking negotiating doesn't mean in order to be successful in sales, you have to be a great negotiator. No, it is possible to be extremely successful in sales without negotiating. The reason is simple—if you're successful in selling, then you don't have to negotiate. Selling is all about getting the Customer to share with you their needs and the benefits they desire. Selling is about you showing the Customer how what you're offering is going to benefit them at a price/value relationship they can understand and appreciate.

If you're accomplishing these things, then there is no need to negotiate with the Customer because there is nothing to negotiate. Negotiation only has to occur when the Customer does not see the full value of the product or service you're offering. If you're doing your job in a superior manner (from a sales perspective), then negotiating is not necessary.

Our perspective is that far too many salespeople jump into negotiating with the Customer too quickly, and the only reason they do so is because they've done a poor job in selling the Customer. When the salesperson does this, the end result only gets worse for them because they start negotiating without even having a clear under-standing of the Customer's needs and desired benefits.

Average and poor salespeople do this as their way of trying to save a sale. Yes, they may close the sale, but they'll do it either at a re-duced price (and reduced profit) or by offering something addi-tional to the Customer. In either case, they've given up something they wouldn't have had to if they had been more successful with their selling process. In both ways, they have not maximized profit.

One quick rule: Unless the Customer has told you at least three needs they have or benefits they desire (with which you know you can help them) there is no sense in even thinking about negotiating. You'll only wind up losing. I've watched too many sales negotia-tions be nothing more than an exercise in futility for one simple reason: the salesperson entering the negotiation was ready to concede any-thing to get the sale. If you think this isn't you, that's fine. You're enti-tled to your belief, but I'll bet my description does actually fit you.

Why? Far too many times, we, as salespeople, will go into a sales negotiation thinking, *"What is it going to take to close the sale?"* The problem is, what we're thinking is usually far less price-wise than what the Customer is thinking. We wind up with a "pre-negotiation mindset" for any number of reasons, but mostly because we simply fail to believe enough in what we're selling and our own sales/ne-gotiating skills. This is the entire reason why we wrote this book— to give you the insights you need so you never find yourself with the "pre-negotiation mindset."

We believe you have to win the sale, but too often "winning" comes at a cost that translates into a huge amount of lost profit. It all comes down to not having a plan and, therefore, not being confident. The level of confidence you having going into a sales meeting or—dare we say it—a negotiating session is going to reflect the level of suc-cess you achieve coming out.

Sell first, negotiate second. We've said it before, but we'll say it again. When you sell first, you're taking the time to understand the Customer and allow them to develop a level of confidence in you, while at the same time, you're developing a level of confidence in yourself.

THE PERFECT NEGOTIATION.
Never walk into a negotiation thinking the outcome is going to be perfect. That is simply an unrealistic expectation.

Here are a couple of things to keep in mind. Nobody gets everything. Warren Buffet hasn't made money on every deal he's made, a baseball player doesn't get a hit every time he is at the plate, and a salesperson doesn't make a sale with every potential Customer.

Part of your plan is to walk into every meeting knowing your minimum and if you're pushed farther than that, you simply walk away. Failure to know when to walk away will only result in making deals that simply have zero merit.

One time an incredibly successful businessperson, whose net worth was measured in the billions, shared with me a quote he used frequently in his companies: "Sometimes the most profitable business is the business you don't get." I will never forget that—and I will never forget the implication. You must know when to walk away.

Too many people go into a negotiation essentially blind, and the worst thing of all is they don't even realize it. They think because they know what they want; they're going to be just fine. Sorry, negotiating is not just understanding what you want; it's also knowing what the other person wants.

When you go into a negotiation not knowing where the other person is coming from with regard to their goals, what they're willing to trade, what they see value in, and what their timeline is for making a decision, then you're essentially going in blind. When this happens, you're likely to end up as their lunch—especially if the other person knows these things about you! The worst thing of all is that when you go into a negotiation blind *and* the other person is incredibly aware, you won't even know what is happening to you until it's too late.

Many times when this happens, the outcome gets even worse, if you can believe it. The person who is not prepared suddenly realizes their disadvantage, and they make haphazard attempts to try to gain the upper hand. The problem is if the other person knows you're blind, then they're going to pick up on it right away and turn it against you.

There are some simple rules you can follow to keep from going into a negotiation blind. They are:

- ☆ Never negotiate with anyone unless you know they have the authority to make the decision.

- ☆ Never negotiate with anyone unless you know his or her timeline for making a decision.

- ☆ Never negotiate with anyone until you know at least three things they value in what you're offering.

- ☆ Never negotiate with anyone until you know his or her sense of a price/value relationship with regard to your customized Solution.

These aren't complicated rules, and if you can objectively answer them before starting to negotiate with the other person, you won't be blind. The chances are that you'll know at least as much as the other person knows, if not more.

Sales negotiation is an activity that can only start after you have first gone through the selling process. The selling process is so important because, in this phase, you can find out the answers to the four rules listed above. If your Customers are controlling sales negotiations, you need a better plan. I'm going to make a safe bet that your Customer is controlling you more than you might think.

Salespeople love to negotiate. We are strong believers that a key weakness in the sales community is that salespeople are too quick to negotiate. Many times, the Customer controls sales more than the salesperson.

Before you doubt us and stop reading, here are a couple of examples:

Have you ever had a Customer who told you they were ready to buy, only to suddenly put off placing an order?

How about the Customer who, just as they're about to buy from you, suddenly asks you about your competitor and their price?

Or what about the Customer who says they'd love to buy from you, but before they'll buy, they will need you to match a competitor's price?

We've all been there, and in each of these cases, the Customer is showing they're in control of your sales negotiations. Statements like these from Customers are going to happen. Don't think you're exempt. The questions or comments your Customer states might not be one of the examples above, but the objective is the same—they want you to cave. Your objective is to not cave to their request or even allow them to think they've thrown you off guard.

The way you immediately respond to them is going to go a long way in determining the Customer's next move. If you don't allow yourself to get rattled, you can often take back control, especially if the Customer is not a seasoned negotiator. I say this because a Customer who is not a strong negotiator may know what to ask for, but they won't know how to respond to any rebuttal.

NEGOTIATE FROM THE RIGHT POSITION.
Also show your calm side. When you look surprised or flustered, you lose control. Use a question to buy you time to consider your response and keep control.

For the Customer who is a seasoned negotiator, it is going to come down to what you choose to say in response to their request. Be ready with a question of your own. When you answer their demand, it puts you in a position of weakness. Asking them a question of your own is a much better way to respond to them. Ask the Customer a question designed to get them thinking about the most critical need they have. By doing this, you are now taking the upper hand.

Sharp negotiators will see this, respect you for it, and realize you're not going to give a quick concession. For the sharp negotiator who knows they need what you're selling, they will quietly concede that you are not going to back down. If the sharp negotiator is not yet sold on what you're offering, then what you've done is bring the negotiation back to a neutral position without giving either side the upper hand.

These may seem like small nuances in sales negotiations, but if you want to be the one in control, you absolutely have to master these techniques. Below is a list that is basically the summary of what it takes to be successful in a negotiating session. Mastering each one of these is not going to guarantee success, but they will dramatically increase your potential for success.

ADVISOR SELLING
NEGOTIATING CHECKLIST

You can refer to the next 12 steps as the "Advisor Selling Negotiating Checklist." As you read through the list, ask yourself how you can apply each one.

1. Never negotiate with anyone who is not qualified to negotiate.

If in doubt, ask how they've handled a similar type of negotiating in the past. Listen for names, dates, and other information that will provide clues as to their level of responsibility.

When you negotiate with someone who is not qualified to negotiate, you're at a huge disadvantage. At no time should you put anything on the table they could then pass along to someone else. If you do find yourself negotiating with someone who is not qualified, you should shift your approach to only looking to obtain information.

2. Never put things into writing unless you're prepared to live with them.

Once an item is put into writing, it becomes an anchor either for you or the Customer.

This is especially critical when negotiating with a professional buyer who will use anything put into writing as leverage. Keep in mind a few simple questions. Are you prepared to have whatever you put into writing shared with the competition? Are you prepared to have a competitor use your information to secure a better deal?

If you do put anything in writing, it must include specific expiration dates as well as information that could be interpreted in several different ways. This gives you the ability to control the way the information is used.

3. Always have room to give something the other person will consider a perceived benefit.

This is why it is so important to sell first and negotiate second. By selling first, you have the opportunity to ask questions and validate the key benefits for which the Customer is looking.

During negotiation, a Customer will attempt to mask the benefits they desire, making it harder to determine exactly what the Customer wants. This continues to emphasize the importance of the selling process. Never enter a negotiation until you have sold first and have heard "no" at least twice. This is why we put the advice for negotiation in the **ANSWER** Phase and not sooner. By going through the selling process first, it will give you the opportunity to uncover the real benefits the Customer wants.

4. Know when to walk away, and be confident in doing so.

To execute this requires the "walk away point" being shared in advance with others in your company to ensure accountability if and when you have to use this tactic.

If you enter into a negotiation without knowing your walk away point, you will be destined to give away more than you should in a final negotiation. Sharing the walk away point with your superior will give you the confidence you need to walk away. If your superior is not in agreement with you about the walk away point, there is little chance you will actually walk away. Instead, you will allow yourself to get "nickel and dimed" into a price lower than you can afford to offer.

5. Know at least five things the other person wants that you can offer.

Again, this is why it is so important to sell first and negotiate second. By doing so, it will be possible to know what can be offered in advance. Negotiations are lost when one party does not have the ability to leverage things the other party wants. When you don't know what the other person is looking for in advance, the process becomes nothing more than extortion.

6. Know at least five things you can say that will discount what the other person is offering (price not included).

Never negotiate on price. Negotiate using other items, such as technical performance, operational efficiencies, delivery arrangements, etc., that will provide the leverage needed to avoid a price-oriented discussion.

The most successful negotiations are those where you have a balance of information, both in terms of what the Customer is looking for and in how you can discount things they might try to ask for. Having your responses developed in advance will allow you to be far more confident when you're in the middle of negotiations and need to respond quickly. Do not attempt to negotiate without first having developed the answers you're going to provide to questions you may be asked. Likewise, be sure to know what questions you're going to ask.

7. Always treat the other person with respect and dignity.

Negotiate over things and services, not personal matters. Never allow the negotiation to become personal in nature.

This even applies to those situations where a close personal relationship may exist. A quick rule to keep in mind: If the relationship is so good, then why is anything being negotiated anyway? If a negotiation does become personal in nature, do not hesitate to step away and arrange a follow-up time to resume the conversation. By adhering to this, you can minimize the potential of the negotiation becoming emotional. Should either you or the other party become emotional at anytime during the negotiation phase, then it is absolutely essential you stop negotiating immediately.

8. Never enter a negotiating process until both sides are clear on what is being negotiated.

At the start of a negotiation, it is appropriate to state exactly what is up for discussion. By doing this up front, it's possible to avoid a waste of time and, more importantly, inadvertently negotiate things that don't need to be discussed. How can you negotiate anything if you don't know what is being negotiated?

PRICE IS NOT AN OPTION.
Keep in mind a negotiation that is only dealing with price is not a negotiation—it's a "blank-check" discussion where the only possible outcome is you losing money.

This is another reason why it is so important for us to spend so much time selling the Customer before entering into negotiation. Spending as much time as possible attempting to close the sale via the Advisor Selling process will allow you to identify what the other party wants. Never attempt to enter into any negotiation without first being able to identify exactly what is being negotiated with the other party. Keep in mind the more things you have to negotiate about, the less the process will focus on price.

9. Use the sell/buy approach first.

The only reason to begin negotiating is if you are unsuccessful closing the sale first. Minimally, no negotiating should begin until the Customer has rejected the close at least twice and the Customer has provided you with at least one buying signal.

Too many salespeople lose the negotiation because they failed to sell first. Professional buyers will always attempt to get to the negotiation phase as soon as possible, especially if they feel they're dealing with a weak salesperson.

10. Never offer options until after you're deadlocked on price, and the Customer has provided you with additional information.

This includes providing you with a buying signal and credible benefits as to what the Customer desires. As soon as something is offered up to the Customer, it becomes incredibly difficult to take it back. Therefore, you have to be cautious about putting anything on the table until you know it is something the Customer wants. You also want them to provide you with additional information.

11. Always put the negotiated outcome in writing immediately.

Do not leave issues open for further discussion. The person who puts the outcomes in writing first wins by being able to position things in the manner they want. Putting things into writing first also provides the opportunity to make one final modification with minimal risk.

The person who puts the information into writing first is the person who will always have the upper hand. This is particularly true if the negotiation process is going to extend over several meetings. When putting the information into writing, it is acceptable to put it in writing as you see it. This then becomes your opening position when the negotiation process resumes.

12. Upon reaching an agreement, thank the other party, but do not celebrate.

Celebrating the outcome of a negotiation sends the signal to the other party that you have taken advantage of them. Sending this signal will jeopardize the long-term potential of the relationship. View every negotiation as if it is merely another step in the long-term process, which it typically is. Celebrating the completion of a negotiation will always leave the other party feeling you "won." It will automatically put you at a disadvantage when the next sale or negotiation begins.

PROCUREMENT AGENT/ PROFESSIONAL BUYER

This book would not be complete without a section on how to deal with the professional buyer. These are the people who you get pushed off to, who believe they're the experts, and who, many times, believe it is their job to be the ultimate roadblock keeping salespeople at bay.

They take on a wide variety of titles, including Purchasing Agent, Procurement Manager, or Supply-Chain Coordinator, but in the end they do similar jobs. Their job, in the simplest terms, is to get the best price they can for everything their company needs.

As simple as it may sound, it's a job that is far more complex. We could write an entire book on this subject, but generally the role they play should not be described as beating up salespeople, but rather as maximizing the return on their investment. When we look at the professional buyer's job as maximizing the return on investment, we can begin to see what it is all about.

For many professional buyers, the easiest part of their day is dealing with salespeople, not because they enjoy beating them up, but rather because of all the attacks they take from others inside the company.

Think about it for a moment. You work for a company and you're used to having "x" to do your job. You like "x" because it's what you've used for years, you're familiar with it, and you know how good it is. Suddenly, you find yourself no longer having "x." Instead, you now have "z," and it's all because the buyer thought "x" was too expensive. What's your reaction? It's to go yell at purchasing for buying "z" when they should know you like "x." Buyers find themselves in this is the type of discussion more often than they will ever admit.

Because of this, you know it's usually a bluff when a buyer says they're going to stop buying from you because your price is too high. Think for a moment about the work a buyer goes through to switch suppliers. Then, think about the number of meetings they're going to be in trying to keep the users calm.

Being a buyer can be a thankless job in any company. When it appears they're taking it all out on salespeople, it may very well be because *they* are often getting beaten up. Let's look at some of the techniques used by professional buyers when they want to take advantage of a salesperson.

It's important that you know these so you will be better equipped to negotiate.

Buyers will...

1. Keep arguing about the price being too high, even if it isn't.

They know salespeople tend to cave under pressure. Because that's the case, it can be easy money. All they have to do is say a price is too high and be willing to argue about it.

2. Always say they have another supplier who can take care of them a lot better.

There are always other suppliers they can switch to, but the last thing they're going to tell a salesperson is the truth. The buyer really doesn't want to switch suppliers because of all the hassle that goes along with switching.

3. Make comments about how every supplier is being told they need to cut their prices by another three percent.

Professional buyers use this approach far too often, and it takes on a number of forms. Some purchasing departments will send letters to all of their vendors. Some will schedule "special meetings" to explain the necessary price cuts, while others will simply bring it up at the start or end of a sales call to catch the salesperson off guard.

The reason buyers love doing this is because it works. Far too many salespeople and companies will roll over and give in to the Customer without any hesitation.

4. State how they have plenty of options to buy on the "grey market" at a much better price.

This is one of the oldest tricks in the book. It may not be the "grey market"; it might be a "third-party supplier" or someone else. The embarrassing thing is far too many companies have side businesses set up selling into "grey markets" or to "third parties," so they're naturally scared when they hear it could come back to bite them.

5. Demand the largest volume discount price on all orders, regardless of size.

Why shouldn't buyers ask for this? They know systems are already set up to handle different prices based on quantities. Many times, a buyer will say they want the volume discount, and if they don't get it, they will merely deduct the amount from the invoice.

6. Not say anything at all, knowing that if they stay silent, the salesperson will sweeten the deal.

Silence is golden and it works both ways. The salesperson that keeps quiet knows they're going to be more effective. Unfortunately, the sharp buyer knows the same thing. The problem is, when the salesperson is sitting in the buyer's office and knows the clock is ticking, they tend to give in by merely blurting out a lower price.

If you are a salesperson who has to work closely with professional buyers, the key is to not become flustered when you hear one of these. If you become anxious and flustered, you will play into the hands of the buyer even more. If you do, the buyer will know it and work you over. Stay calm and resolute in your offer.

Professional buyers will back off if they see you're not moving. Their objective isn't to take advantage of you, even if it does feel that. Their objective is to help reduce the cost of buying for their company.

We're not sharing these insights out of disrespect to professional buyers. The entire reason buyers can say any of these at all is because they've seen salespeople rollover and give in.

Remember, the professional buyer is only doing his or her job. Your job is to be the professional salesperson and sell to the Customer's needs and outcomes, be confident in your job and price, and protect your profit.

PROFESSIONAL BUYERS.
Remember, it's not personal, it's just business. These people can frustrate you if you let them. Understand their role and practice extra patience.

Over the years, I've had the opportunity work closely with a number of buying departments, many times as part of the sales training I'm doing for their salespeople.

Here are just a few of the many confessions I've heard from professional buyers:

My goal is to always keep the face-to-face meetings short.

Keeping meetings short helps keep the salesperson guessing, and when they start guessing, they tend to offer better deals. Just as the salesperson is about to leave the office, I always make one more quick request to test them and to put even more doubt about me in their mind.

Making demands via voicemail is a great way to can get more from the salesperson.

Making demands using voicemail prevents the salesperson from trying to counter the demand. By not putting it in writing, it also allows for last minute changes to get an even better deal.

This one hurts, because I personally fell victim to it early in my sales career. As a new salesperson, I was eager to make an impression. I felt I could do it by delivering excellent customer service. The problem was the customer service I was giving was in the form of concessions. It didn't take long for the Customer to know they could make demands of me when I was sitting across the desk from them—and also by way of voicemail.

One buyer, in particular, took advantage of me by always leaving me a voicemail 10 minutes after I left his office. I don't even want to calculate how much I cost my company—and to think it was all because I thought I was doing the right thing.

When I am slow to respond to a salesperson's email or phone call, they start to feel like I'm not interested.

The longer it takes me to respond, the more the salesperson will come to believe the offer they made is not good enough. Simply waiting a couple of days to respond to an email can often scare the salesperson into believing the offer isn't good enough.

I'm not going to put anything in writing unless I absolutely have to.

When something is put in writing, it eliminates the ability to make last-minute changes to get even more out of the salesperson. At the same time, however, I always demand the salesperson put everything in writing to give me the power of knowledge, so I can use it against them.

It's great to make the salesperson believe I'm considering multiple vendors.

Even if there is not another vendor, the salesperson doesn't need to know it. Just by saying things like, "we'll compare it with the others," I know I can usually get a better price from the salesperson. No matter how much I may want to do business with them, I don't let them get that sense from me.

Slow is better. I never admit I'm in a rush to buy anything.

Salespeople always believe a slow buyer is an unmotivated buyer. It is amazing how the offer will get better when I take my time making a decision.

NINE

ADVISE PHASE

Truth be told, the sales process has historically ended here. After all, the goal is to make a sale and at this point you have accomplished that goal. But this sales process was written for today's selling climate, which means that there is more work to do if you want to maximize the sale with the Customer.

Now this is a fun place to be in the sale. The Customer has said yes and signed the contract or issued the PO. Now, you have to deliver on the Solution you promised them during the sale and begin preparing for future sales and embedding you and your Solution deep into the Customer account.

WHAT HAVE YOU DONE FOR ME LATELY?

The only good sale is one that leads to the next sale. Having this type of mindset will keep you focused on making sure each sales call you make is the best it can be.

Salespeople who feel their work is done when they deliver the PO are not people we would want on our sales team. The **ADVISE** Phase is where you, the sales professional, either help make incremental profit or contribute to the process of giving up profit.

Let's break this down to allow you to see why this phase is so important. First let's look at the issue of giving up profit. This happens far too often because, during the selling process, the salesperson established expectations with the Customer that were not deliverable.

A few years back, I was working with a company that was struggling to make their numbers. After doing a deep dive into the business, we found it was due to two big reasons. One, was the amount of re-work and handholding that went on with the Customer after they made the purchase. The second the low percentage of repeat Customers. The problem was obvious. The sales team was being beat up so hard to deliver their sales quota, they were making wild commitments to the Customer to get them to buy.

If the sales team continued doing what they were doing, any chance of success the company had would be gone. The solution to the problem came when we recommended the sales team move to an account manager structure, making them responsible for each Customer they brought on board for as long as they were a Customer. It didn't take long for the problem to correct itself. The company went on to achieve a high degree of success because the sales team was now focused on creating Customers for life.

Incremental profits are also a key outcome from this Phase because of the ability to take the information learned during the **PRESENT** Phase and using it now to "wow" the Customer by delivering on their expected outcomes. One could argue that this practice, in itself, doesn't create incremental profit—and they'd be right—it doesn't. But when a Customer is wowed by what they're getting from your company, his receptiveness to buy again and to give a referral for another sale goes WAY up.

Now, we hope you see the importance of the **ADVISE** Phase and what it can do for your business. We would argue that when an organization is optimizing the **ADVISE** Phase, delivering year-over-year growth at an increasing margin, it becomes very doable.

There are two steps in the ADVISE Phase:

1. Educate
2. Evangelize

EDUCATE

There are actually two people you have to Educate in this Phase—your external Customer (the one who you sold to) and your internal Customer (your operations/support team). Both are incredibly important in this process, as either one can lose this sale or keep the next sale from happening. First, let's talk about the internal Customer, since they are the next contact with your Customer.

A best practice here is to make notes in the CRM record of the Customer for the "delivery" team in your company. If you do not have a CRM, then put it into a document and circulate it to the team. Title the document: "How to Delight _____."

Professional services, technical support, delivery, operations, customer care…all of these departments need to know *why* the Customer bought this Solution from your company. Then—and only then—can they affirm the decision.

When working with companies, a great part of our research was not just with the sales teams, but with the Customers these sales teams are calling on.

Here are some of the questions we ask:

> *Why did you buy from_____?*
>
> *What was it about the Solution or company that made you say yes?*
>
> *What are the most important criteria you consider when making a buying decision?*
>
> *How was this experience different from your other partners?*

And then we also ask,

> *What is your biggest frustration after the sale has been made?*
>
> *What advice would you give the company for next time?*

On this last one, we constantly get the same feedback—"it was like working with two different companies" or "The salesperson was awesome. We even met his boss, but after the installation, we never saw them again, and whenever we have a question or an issue, it's always with someone who does not know our situation. I have to explain our situation EVERY time I call in and that takes 10 minutes in itself."

Sound familiar? We are sure it does. Unfortunately, it's too common these days. But, it can be avoided if you Educate your internal Customers. One company we worked with implemented this process by spending every Monday morning with the heads of each department and the sales team in a room going over the "How to Delight" documents for each new Customer. It made a HUGE difference in the Customer satisfaction and protected the "trusted advisor" status of the sales professionals and account managers in the company.

LEAD BLOCKER.
You can invest a ton of personal time in becoming a trusted advisor only to have it all go wrong at the finish line. Do not hand the ball off at the goal line—be the lead blocker into the end zone.

For the external Customer—the one you just made a sale to—the number one reason Customers experience buyer's remorse (where they are second-guessing their decision to buy your Solution) is because they do not fully understand how to use your Solution. Remember our example earlier in this book about what percent of features a Customer may actually use of your Solution? It is your responsibility to make sure that your Customer understands how to get the most benefit out of those features.

Yes, for many of you, you have a "fulfillment" or installation or de-livery team that takes it from there. But if you "let go" and leave the rest of the sale to them, you are risking your chance to get them to Evangelize for you. Let's explain. Rarely, does the fulfillment person know which key features you focused on in your Solution for the Customer. These features are the ones the Customer will work with first. Only you know what the Customer's "hot buttons" are and you need to make sure these are "pushed" during the start of service or install.

Perhaps your product does not need installation. Perhaps you are selling a service and not a product at all. Well, this still applies to you. Even services have multiple offerings or ways to deliver the service with only one or two of those ways being the ones that get the Customer excited about their decision and ready to Evangelize for you. Do you remember our guaranteed on-time delivery exam-ple? If that was a core linchpin for the sale, then that better be the first priority of your company in delivering service. If instead, your implementation team starts with things that are important to them (you know, train the Customer how to do things they way *they* want it done) versus focusing on what was important to the Customer during the sales process, you put your trusted advisor status at risk.

Ultimately, the reason you need an evangelist on your side is not only for new business, but often times, it's to keep the business you have. In today's world, where directors are often given the mandate to "cut their budgets 10%" by their boss, the following scene plays out. Your Customer's director asks all of his direct reports to con-sider cuts and then gather together in the conference room (where all great thinking happens) to discuss and make recommendations. At the meeting, a list of possible cuts is placed on the board, and your company is one on that list! Now, keep in mind, you are not in the room, so there is nothing you can do here. Enter your evangelist (you know, the one you mapped out in the earlier phase of the sale).

If you have evangelist in the room, he or she will fight for you. They will explain your value and work to keep your name off the list of cuts. You see, here is where all of our previous sales techniques will come to bear fruit for you. Remember explaining the Business Fit? We cannot tell you how many deals have been saved because someone did a good job explaining the Business Fit to his or her Customer.

When the room asks why to keep you, your evangelist ready. They can relate the Business Fit and take the conversation well beyond the features and benefits of your product or service (which is how the rest of the room will argue for their items on the list since they were sold, and not advised).

EVANGELIZE

So, we have been using this word a lot in the last few pages, but what does it mean? Simple: if you want a long-term relationship with an account, you need employees of your Customer to become Evangelists for you. An evangelist is a person who seeks to "convert" others to a way of doing things. So, in our example, an Evangelist is the person who gets everyone in the company using your service.

For example, let's say you are selling recycling services. The important thing for you is that the Customer recycles ALL of the materials in their workplace that qualify. But, many people don't care about recycling so they will simply throw their recyclables in with the rest of the trash. That is lost opportunity for you. So, you need some Evangelists inside to get more employees recycling.

You have more competition today than ever before. And sometimes your competition is your Customer. Think about it: if someone does not understand how to get the most out of your Solution, they will stop using it or use it begrudgingly. In either case, they will tell others about their dissatisfaction. Then, others join in and the competition comes knocking on the door and everyone is ready to switch. Getting the picture?

We have seen this happen time and time again. You spend hours and hours to get the sale and then no time to keep it. "But, I don't have time," you say. We get that. That is why you need Evangelists to do it for you.

Recently, I was asked in a session what percent of my business comes from referrals. Honestly, I had not done any study on this— I just worked (not good technique on my part). As I took the time to analyze, it quickly became evident is that the number was about 90%. What was more remarkable was the amount of business that came from referrals of people who I had not done work with in years—they still remembered me and told my story. That certainly sounds like evangelism at its best.

Remember the conference room story a few pages ago? If the evangelist is absent, your business is toast. The room will turn on you and you will get that dreaded phone call telling you they are cancelling your service. You remember it from chapter one, "its not you its me. I just need to see other people [vendors]."

If you are a sales manager reading this book, it's important to pay close attention to the principles laid out in this section with regards to the **ADVISE** Phase. Too many sales managers fail to see the impact and we have yet to see an organization do the **ADVISE** Phase well if the sales manager has not embraced it first. It's really not possible.

The two easiest things you can do as a sales manager are, first, measuring the change in profit that occurs from when a sale is first made to when it is completed. Is it going down? If so, why? The second is to look at the percent of business in your company that comes from referrals and / or repeat sales. Is it changing over time? If so, why? If you're not measuring these things now, chances are you're giving up profit in both.

BEING A TRUSTED ADVISOR.
If you want to be a trusted advisor, you cannot act like a salesman.

As the title of the Phase suggests, you move from the installed start-of-service part of the sale to the trusted advisor part. Here are some tips to maintain trusted advisor status:

⭐ **Have a regular rhythm of "business review" meetings** with your key accounts. Talk about what is working and what is not. Adjust. But more importantly, Interview during these meetings to listen for other opportunities for your company to make the "next" sale. (It's called prospecting if you have been paying attention.)

⭐ **Have a regular rhythm of contact** with your key accounts that does not involve your Solution or your company, but rather their (the Customer's) business.

For example, if you find a great article on quality practices, clip it and send it to your accounts. This communication from you as their advisor adds tremendous value. Even if they never read one article or note you send them, they know you care, and that is what matters. One note on this practice—be sparing. Do not become a pest with junk mail and spam. Only send content that's relevant to your Customer.

⭐ **Invite them to a conference with you.** Pay for the ticket and go with them. Take a group of your accounts together. It's okay. Or perhaps they need CEUs and you put together a class for them to earn them.

135

⭐ **Never leave them as the "problem solver."** I have lost count of the number of times I have seen the last interaction between a salesperson and the Customer going something like this—"Here is my card. If you have any problems, just give me a call." That is not a business card—that is a warranty card! You are the trusted advisor, not the service department. This may sound simple, but it makes a big difference.

There you have it.

Advisor Selling mapped out in detail for you. As we stated in the Introduction, we wrote this book for sales professionals, not sales-people. Sales professionals already have a skill set they bring to the table. We wanted to add some clubs for your bag—not teach you to golf. We went deep on ideas we think are new or important and stayed shallow on areas in which we think you already excel.

But as you finish this book, here are some closing thoughts for you. First, thank you for your attention. It is an honor to have it. We know you have a choice with what to do with your time, and we are glad you invested part of your valuable time with us.

Second, we want to challenge you to work on these principles—to try them fervently and not give up easily. They will take time and they will be challenging, but they do work. We have over 50 years of combined experience to prove it.

I did some work for a golf retailer one time. To thank me for the work, they gave me a set of custom at golf clubs. I flew to Chicago to meet with their PGA pro to fit me for my clubs. It was a tremendous experience. I remember the pro asking me how many wedges I wanted. I wasn't sure how to respond since in my golf life there were only two wedges, a pitching wedge and a sand wedge, and honestly—I only ever used one.

The pro explained to me that there are several different wedges, each with a different "loft." The higher the degree of loft, the higher the flight of the ball. So, the closer to the pin I was, the more loft I needed, since the best shot on the green comes from high and drops onto the green (versus low and runs onto the green). In the second scenario (my normal shot) the ball tends to run by the hole and sometimes off the green. Truth be told, my golf game really only needed one wedge, but I left the store that day with four. The reason? The more clubs, the more accurate the shot (provided I learn to use them well.) The same is true with your sales game. All of the skills that we discussed in Advisor Selling are meant to be "added" to your bag, not necessarily replace what's already in your bag.

If we are honest, the very fact that you are investing your valuable time in reading this book puts you in a different class than most salespeople. You are trying to improve. You are trying to grow. This means you already have some good clubs in your bag. The weak sales person doesn't take the time to invest. They give up and move on but that's just not you. We hope that this book has been worthy of your attention and that there are parts that will help make you a more powerful sales professional. Selling is a profession, a career.

Just as elite athletes have to train in order to be a ready for the big game, you have to train to be ready for the big sale. Remember our story about the quarterback on a football team?

We applaud you for what you're doing by reading this book. We applaud you for practicing the principles that you're learning here, putting them into your bag and making them part of your game. It's our sincere desire that it improves your selling life, your professional life, and your personal life.

At the end of the day, sales is all about helping people achieve things they didn't think were possible. This might be accomplished by helping them avoid a problem. It might be helping them fix an issue, or it might be helping them see things differently for the first time. Regardless of the reason, it's about helping people.

At the end of every training session or speech I give, I always share with the audience that our goal each day is to earn the right, the privilege, the honor, and the respect to be able to meet with them again. For us, that is what makes sales such a wonderful profession. We don't see it as work; we see it as an opportunity to be a positive influence on everyone we meet with.

Happy selling!

REFERENCES AND CITATIONS

CHAPTER 1 — THE APPROACH

[1] Neil Rackham. *Spin Selling.* McGraw Hill, 1988

[2] Various studies completed by a number of organizations including the United States Golf Association (USGA) citing scores when all rules of golf are followed and all strokes counted according to USGA rules.

[3] Research study conducted by Rick Segel Group 2013

CHAPTER 2 — PLAN

[4] Research study conducted by Rick Segel Group 2013

[5] Publishers Weekly

[6] The H.F.Pitzer Study on "Forgetting Meaningful Information."

[7] The National Centre for Reading Education and Research, University of Stavange, Norway and the Mediterranean Institute for Cognitive Neuroscience, CNRS, Université de la Méditerranée, France.

[8] Steven Covey. *7 Habits of Highly Effective People.* DC Books, 2005

CHAPTER 4 — PREPARE

[9] Research study conducted by Rick Segel Group 2013

CHAPTER 5 — PRESENT

[10] Zig Ziglar. *Ziglar on Selling. The Ultimate Handbook for the Complete Sales Professional.* Thomas Nelson, 2003

[11] Gartner Research

[12] The Sales Board. "5 Secrets to Record Breaking Sales" 2013

CHAPTER 6 — PLAY

[13] Chip Heath, Dan Heath *Made to Stick* Random House, 2007

CHAPTER 7 — ASK

[14] Mark Shonka, Dan Kosch, *Beyond Selling Value.* Kaplan Publishing, 2002

CHAPTER 8 — ANSWER

[15] Tom Hopkins. *How to Master the Art of Selling.* Champion, 1982

About the Authors

MATTHEW HUDSON started as a part-time sales associate in Sear's in 1983. Through his 26 years in retail, Matt has managed a store with himself and a part-timer working bell-to-bell 7 days a week (we've all been there), opened over 200 stores, been a Director of Stores for a 3,000 employee, $700M chain, a COO of a 17 store, $70M chain and even owned his own 4-store chain in Fort Worth, Texas, Matt is the president and COO of the Rick Segel Group of companies. He is an award- winning designer, speaker and author of three 3 books including *The Retail Sales Bible*. He has presented speeches on four continents and is a frequent guest columnist on best practices for sales marketing and management.

Prior to joining Rick Segel Group, he was a principal for eight years in the consulting firm, Penumbra Group, Inc. based out of New Hampshire. While there, he worked with Fortune 50 companies and helped small, emergent companies make the leap from entrepreneurialism to true corporations. His clients include Dell (where he was the lead retail strategy consultant,) New Balance, Life Fitness, Hyatt Regency, Disney, Golf Galaxy, RadioShack and many more.

For more information about Matt, **visit** <u>ricksegel.com</u> or Follow him on Twitter — @hudsonhead

Or download the app on your Android, Windows or iOS device

Just scan the QR Code and be directed to your app store.

MARK HUNTER, "The Sales Hunter," is recognized as one of the Top 50 Most Influential Sales and Marketing Leaders in the world. He helps companies identify better prospects, close more sales, and profitably build more long-term customer relationships. As a sales expert, he speaks to thousands each year on how to increase their sales profitability.

Mark specializes in customized training programs and keynotes on sales. He is best known for his thorough understanding of pricing strategies and sales leadership. From the CEO to the front-line sales team, organizations look to Mark to help them develop profitable outcomes.

He spent more than 18 years in the sales and marketing divisions of three Fortune 100 companies. During his career, he led many projects, including the creation of a new 200-member sales force responsible for volume in excess of $700 million. This level of experience is at the core of the many programs he delivers each year in the areas of sales, communication and leadership.

Since 1998, Mark has advised sales teams at numerous companies, including Coca-Cola, Heineken, Kawasaki, Mattel, Dole and American Express. He is author of the best-selling book, *High-Profit Selling: Win the Sale Without Compromising on Price.* In it he outlines many of the specific techniques sales teams can use to accelerate sales motivation and protect profits.

With a keen ability to motivate organizations through his high-energy presentations, Mark customizes his programs to his clients' unique industries and needs. His success is seen in his schedule, as he globally travels more than 200 days per year speaking at conferences and working with salespeople and sales leaders.

You can find out more about Mark at **www.TheSalesHunter.com**, where he blogs regularly on the critical issues impacting sales and leadership.

Other Books By Matthew & Mark
To Order call 800.814.7998

The Retail Sales Bible
The G.R.E.A.T. Selling System for Retail
$19.95

Culturrifc!
The Roadmap to Building a Cuturiffic!
Service Team Matt's thesis on creating a
service-oriented corporate culture.
$19.95

Signs Sell
Harnessing the Power of Your Interior
Advertising
$25.95

High-Profit Selling
Win the Sale Without Compromising
the Price
$19.95

10386878R00086

Printed in Great Britain
by Amazon.co.uk, Ltd.,
Marston Gate.